Great Lakes, Great Breakfasts
A Cookbook & Travel Guide

From the
Innkeepers of the
Michigan Lake to Lake
Bed & Breakfast
Association

D1285020

The
Guest
Cottage Inc.
Woodruff, Wisconsin

Copyright © 2002 The Guest Cottage, Inc.

First Edition

All rights reserved. Reproduction in whole or in part of any
portion in any form without permission of publisher is
prohibited.

The Guest Cottage, Inc.
PO Box 848
Woodruff, WI 54568
1-800-333-8122
Please call or write for a free catalog of other books by
the Guest Cottage.

ISBN#: 1-930596-10-3

Printed in the United States of America

Marketed by The Guest Cottage, Inc.
Cover art by Kathleen Parr McKenna ~ www.kpmdesign.com
Designed by Debra Adams

Contents

Participating Inns

State Map of Participating Cities

Guide by City of Participating Inns

Bed & Breakfast
Profiles and Recipes

Castle in the Country
Bed & Breakfast

340 M-40 South
Allegan, MI 49010
(888)673-8054
www.castleinthecountry.com
ruth@castleinthecountry.com

Hosts: Herb and Ruth Boven

Enchanting evenings begin at our Victorian country castle. We'll pamper you with in-room or dining room presented breakfasts. Whirlpools, fireplaces and beautiful surroundings delight your senses and refresh your spirit. Our adventure map will pinpoint specially referred restaurants, activities and pastimes. Or spend your visit happily "nesting" in our romantic guest rooms. All rooms have TV/VCRs, air conditioning and plush details for your enjoyment. Several rooms have whirlpool tubs and fireplaces.

Don't miss our website for virtual tour photos, midweek/off-season specials, murder mystery/romance packages and on-line availability and booking. Nearby you'll find fine dining, wineries, antiques, biking, golf and downhill/cross-country skiing. It's a short 30 minutes to Saugatuck, Holland, South Haven and Kalamazoo.

Rates at Castle in the Country range from $85-$185.
Rates include a full breakfast.

Royal Eggs & Cheese

Treat yourself and your breakfast guests royally with this cheesy show stopper. Make as many or as few individual servings as needed. Serve with fresh fruit or flower garnish, maple flavored link sausage and toast tips.

individual serving

1/2 cup shredded Cheddar cheese, divided
1 baking potato, thinly sliced
1 teaspoon red pepper, finely chopped
1/8 teaspoon garlic salt or to taste
1 Tablespoon half-and-half
1 large egg
nonstick cooking spray

1 small mixing bowl
1 microwaveable plate
1 individual serving tart pan or glass ramekin
Baking Time: 15-20 minutes
Baking Temperature: 400°

Preheat oven to 400°. Spray tart pan with nonstick cooking spray. Sprinkle 1/4 cup Cheddar cheese to fill half full.

Peel and slice one baking potato and place on microwaveable plate. Spray with nonstick cooking spray to coat and sprinkle with garlic salt to taste. Microwave on baked potato setting.

Place baked potato slices, usually 3-4 slices per serving, in a layer over cheese. Layer red pepper over potatoes. Sprinkle with cheese to cover peppers.

In a small mixing bowl, mix egg with half-and-half. Pour mixture over cheese. Sprinkle with garlic salt to taste. Layer with remaining cheese.

Bake for 15-20 minutes at 400°. Remove from oven and blot excess oil from top of pan. Invert onto serving plate.

Saravilla
Bed & Breakfast

633 North State Street
Alma, MI 48801
(989)463-4078
www.saravilla.com
ljdarrow@saravilla.com

Hosts: Linda and Jon Darrow

If you are interested in historic and unique, have we got a Bed & Breakfast for you! Our 11,000 square foot mansion, full of original features, was built in 1894 as a summer cottage for a very self-indulged young woman, who was the sole surviving child of a wealthy lumber baron. We are centrally located in our state and on the way to everywhere! We also provide a very peaceful, quiet setting for just getting away. You can enjoy wood-burning fireplaces, a hot tub, a whirlpool, ping pong or billiards, piano, a wraparound front porch and an English garden with a pond. We are only two blocks from downtown and only 18 miles to a large casino.

Rates at Saravilla Bed & Breakfast range from $85-$140.
Rates include a full breakfast.

Cheesy Potato Oven Omelets

This is a great recipe for a variety of reasons: it is a bit different than the typical breakfast dish, it's easy to fix, it can be fixed ahead, and it can be prepared in various size dishes to serve small or large groups. It stores well, freezes well, reheats well and can be adjusted for a meatless dish. Guests consistently ask for this recipe.

serves 10-12

2 cups frozen hash brown potatoes, thawed
1 pound cooked sausage, ham, or smoked sausage, drained
8 ounces Monterey Jack cheese
2 cans (8 ounces each) Durkee onions, crumbled
1 Tablespoon minced parsley, fresh or dried
8 large eggs
1 1/2 cups milk
1 1/2 teaspoons crushed rosemary
1/2 teaspoon pepper
1 teaspoon salt (optional)

1 large mixing bowl
1 medium mixing bowl
1 - 9 x 13 inch baking dish
Baking Time: 1 hour
Baking Temperature: 350°

Preheat oven to 350°. In a large mixing bowl, combine potatoes, meat, cheese, onions and parsley. In a medium mixing bowl, blend together eggs, milk, rosemary, salt and pepper. Pour egg mixture over potato mixture and mix together. Pour into a greased 9 x 13 inch baking dish. Bake at 350° for 1 hour. Let stand 5 minutes before serving.

Arcadia House
Bed & Breakfast

17304 Sixth Street
Arcadia, MI 49613
(231) 889-4394
www.thearcadiahouse.com
innfo@thearcadiahouse.com

Hosts: Phyllis and David Baldwin

Forested hillsides presenting outstanding Lake Michigan views surround the picturesque port village of Arcadia. Our turn of the century home is fully air conditioned and offers five guest rooms, each with private bath. Antique furnishings and appointments throughout create a sense of grace and elegance – a welcome escape from the hurried pace of modern life. Enjoy a cozy fire in the formal parlor, table games with other guests in the sitting room, or birding from our front porch swing. A gourmet breakfast served with fine china and glowing silver is a great start for your vacation day! Centrally located between Sleeping Bear Lakeshore and Manistee National Forest, Arcadia House is your gateway to Northwest Michigan's all season vacationland. Spectacular scenery, country charm, unforgettable sunsets, and starry nights – no charge!

Rates at Arcadia House range from $85-$95.
Rates include a full breakfast.

Crimson Pears

This is a great recipe to use when fresh, local fruits are no longer available. It is easy to make, adds color to the table, and is sure to delight you and your guests!

serves 6

---

3 medium fresh pears
3/4 cup water
1 cup sugar
1 teaspoon vanilla

Cranberry Sauce:
1 1/2 cups cranberries
Reserved syrup

1- 3 quart saucepan
6 sauce dishes or pretty glass bowl

Peel, core, and half pears. Mix water, sugar and vanilla in 3 quart saucepan. Add pears to pan and simmer about 20 minutes until tender but still firm. Reserve the syrup. Remove from pan and place in serving dishes.

Cranberry Sauce:
Add cranberries to vanilla syrup in saucepan. Cook cranberries over medium heat until cranberries pop. Stir and let cool. Spoon cranberries over pears and serve.

Keswick Manor
A Luxury City Inn

1800 Center Avenue
Bay City, MI 48708
(989)893-6598
www.keswickmanor.com
keswickmanor@aol.com

Hosts: Tom and Debbie Pietrzak

Welcome to Keswick Manor, a luxury city inn. Your stay will be special in every way. We offer unsurpassed service, exquisite food and elegant suites. Conveniently located near the downtown Bay City riverfront, shopping and restaurants are a short distance from our door. This beautiful, historic 1896 Georgian inn is filled with antiques and English inspired accessories. The grounds have many gardens and fountains. You will be pampered with endless amenities and luxuries. Keswick Manor takes elegance to its highest level.

Rates at Keswick Manor range from $89-$189.
Rates include a full breakfast.

Cranberry & Oatmeal Muffins

Our guests at Keswick Manor love these muffins hot out of the oven on chilly autumn mornings! I have been making these muffins for years, and everyone wants more to take home when they check out!

makes 1 dozen muffins

3/4 cup all-purpose flour
3/4 cup whole wheat flour
1 cup oatmeal (do not use quick or instant oatmeal)
1/2 cup brown sugar
1 Tablespoon baking powder
1 teaspoon salt
1 teaspoon cinnamon
1 cup frozen cranberries
1/2 cup chopped walnuts
1/4 cup (1/2 stick) real butter
1 cup milk
1 egg

2 small mixing bowls
2 muffin pans (regular size)
Baking Time: 15-20 minutes
Baking Temperature: 425°

Preheat oven to 425°. Butter muffin cups.

In a small mixing bowl, combine dry ingredients and blend well.

Toss cranberries and walnuts with 1 Tablespoon of dry ingredients. Set aside.

Melt butter. Remove from heat and stir in milk and egg. Stir butter mixture into dry ingredients. When well mixed, stir in cranberries and walnuts.

Bake 15-20 minutes until lightly browned. Let stand for 5 minutes before removing from pan.

Serve with vanilla yogurt.

The Elliott House Bed & Breakfast

7099 Crystal Avenue
P.O. Box 53
Beulah, MI 49617
(231) 882-7075
www.elliottbb.com
delliott@bignetnorth.net

Hosts: Diane and Pat Elliott

The Elliott House is located in the heart of Benzie County where Northern Michigan preserved holds true. Located in the village of Beulah, across from Crystal Lake, we offer three rooms, each decorated to reflect Northern Michigan and all with private baths and televisions. Views of Crystal Lake can be enjoyed from any room in our home, and we have a spacious common area, where the cookie jar is always full and our player piano is ready to play some of your favorite tunes.

Our wraparound front porch offers relaxation after spending the day discovering the many family and adult attractions, including Sleeping Bear Dunes National Lakeshore, Pt. Betsie Lighthouse, antique shops, golf courses, wineries, biking Benzie County's Rails to Trails, Lake Michigan beaches, and canoeing and tubing the Platte or Betsie rivers. When was the last time you saw a drive-in movie? One of Michigan's oldest is only 5 minutes away, and Crystal Lake Beach is across the street from our home.

Rates at The Elliott House range from $79-$99.
Rates include a continental plus breakfast.

Blueberry Buckle

Northern Michigan blueberries, fresh or frozen, makes this buckle easy to enjoy year-round.

serves 6

3/4 cup sugar
1/4 cup butter or margarine
2 eggs
1 teaspoon vanilla
2 cups flour
2 teaspoons baking powder
1/2 teaspoon salt
1/2 cup buttermilk
2 1/2 cups fresh or frozen blueberries

Topping:
1/4 cup sugar
1/4 cup packed brown sugar
1/4 cup flour
1/4 cup butter or margarine
1/2 teaspoon ground cinnamon

1 small mixing bowl
1 medium mixing bowl
1 large mixing bowl
1- 9-inch square baking dish

Baking Time: 30-40 minutes
Baking Temperature: 375°

Cream sugar and butter; beat in eggs and vanilla. Combine flour, baking powder and salt. Add flour mixture and buttermilk alternately to batter. Stir in berries. Spread in a lightly greased 9 inch-square baking dish.

Topping:
Blend topping ingredients until crumbly. Sprinkle on batter.

Bake at 375° for 30-40 minutes or until toothpick comes out clean.

Dewey Lake Manor
Bed & Breakfast

11811 Laird Road
Brooklyn, MI 49230
(517) 467-7122
www.getaway2smi.com/dewey
deweylk@frontiernet.net

Hosts: Joe and Barb Phillips

Sitting atop a knoll overlooking Dewey Lake, a "country retreat" awaits manor guests in the Irish Hills of Southern Michigan. This Italianate-style house was built by A.F. Dewey, a prosperous farmer of the area who owned the lake and all the land around it. This century-old home, furnished with antiques and original kerosene chandeliers, is a quiet, peaceful place to enjoy the sweet sounds of summer nights or the quiet stillness of the frozen lake. There are five bedrooms with fireplaces and private baths, and guests may enjoy the paddleboat, canoe, picnics and bonfires. There is golf and antiquing nearby.

Rates at Dewey Lake Manor range from $72-$130.
Rates include a full breakfast.

Frittata for Two

This recipe was shared with me by a former Bed and Breakfast owner. Serving 2 or 4 people "something different" can sometimes be hard. This frittata solved the problem and it's so easy!

serves 2

---

1 sausage link, cut into small pieces
3 eggs
1/4 cup cream or half-and-half
1/4 cup Colby cheese, shredded
4 ounces shredded hash brown potatoes, frozen
1 teaspoon diced red pepper
1 teaspoon diced green pepper
1 teaspoon (or less) minced onion – can use dried onion
salt & pepper to taste

1 medium mixing bowl
1 small mixing bowl
1- 6-inch ovenproof skillet (I use an antique Pyrex with snap off handle)
Baking Time: 25-35 minutes
Baking Temperature: 350°

Brown sausage link in a small skillet sprayed with nonstick cooking spray. Set aside. Whisk eggs well in a medium mixing bowl. Add remaining ingredients to eggs, including sausage. Pour into greased ovenproof skillet. Bake uncovered for 25-35 minutes until just set. Cut into 4 wedges and serve. I serve it with fresh baked cinnamon rolls and bacon or sausage patties on the side.

Waterloo Gardens
Bed & Breakfast

7600 Werkner Road
Chelsea, MI 48118
(734)433-1612
www.waterloogardensbb.com
waterloogardens@prodigy.com

Host: Lourdean Offenbacher

Waterloo Gardens Bed & Breakfast is a modern two story ranch home located in beautiful Chelsea, close to Waterloo Recreation Area and Ann Arbor. We're just five minutes from downtown Chelsea and the famous Common Grill and Purple Rose Theater. Stroll the lovely gardens or relax on the deck. Let the master spa's heated jets melt away the stresses of the week. Play a game of pool or watch a video or DVD on the big screen television. Work out in the fitness center. Choose from three decorated guest rooms. There are a lot of common areas in which to hang out.

Our inn is smoke free, and we have two (very friendly) Golden Retrievers. A hearty and delicious breakfast is served daily. Relax and enjoy.

Rates at Waterloo Gardens range from $85-$135.
Rates include a full breakfast.

Cranberry Oatmeal Cookies

Dotted with cranberries, orange peel and vanilla chips, these cookies are so colorful and fun to eat. They look lovely on a dessert tray.

makes 6 dozen cookies

---

1 cup butter or margarine, softened
1 1/2 cups sugar
2 eggs
1 teaspoon vanilla extract
2 cups all-purpose flour
1 teaspoon baking powder
1/2 teaspoon salt
1/4 teaspoon baking soda
2 cups quick-cooking or regular oats
1 cup raisins or dried cranberries (I prefer craisins)
1 cup coarsely chopped fresh or frozen cranberries
1 Tablespoon orange peel, grated
1 package (12 ounces) vanilla chips

2 medium mixing bowls
1 cookie sheet
wire racks
Baking Time: 10-12 minutes
Baking Temperature: 375°

Preheat oven to 375°. In a medium mixing bowl, cream butter and sugar. Add eggs, one at a time, beating well after each addition. Beat in vanilla. In another bowl, combine flour, baking powder, salt and baking soda; add to the creamed mixture. Stir in oats, raisins, cranberries and orange peel. Stir in vanilla chips. Drop by rounded teaspoonsful 2 inches apart on greased baking sheet.

Bake at 375° for 10-12 minutes or until edges are lightly browned.

Cool on wire racks.

Another great recipe from Waterloo Gardens Bed & Breakfast...

White Chocolate-Nut Bars

This delicious recipe is fun and easy to make! Use the variations listed below to give the recipe a different taste or experiment on your own!

makes 32 bars

---

1 package Super Moist butter recipe chocolate cake mix
1/2 cup (1 stick) margarine or butter, melted
1/2 cup brown sugar
2 Tablespoons water
1 egg
1 cup chopped walnuts
1 package (10 ounces) vanilla milk chips

1 large mixing bowl
1- 9 x 13 x 2-inch pan
Baking Time: 32-36 minutes
Baking Temperature: 350 °

Preheat oven to 350 °. Grease rectangular 9 x 13 x 2-inch pan. Mix cake mix (dry), margarine, brown sugar, water and egg in a large mixing bowl, using spoon. Stir in walnuts and vanilla milk chips.

Press firmly in pan. Bake 32-36 minutes or until top forms a crust that is dry to the touch.

Cool completely. Cut into 2 x 1 1/2 inch bars.

Flavors of cake mix, chips and nuts may be substituted.
I like to use yellow cake mix and white and chocolate chips. I then frost the bars with chocolate fudge frosting.

Another great recipe from Waterloo Gardens Bed & Breakfast...

Peach French Toast

Your guests will love this tasty, easy recipe. Prepare it the night before; enjoy it the next morning with friends and family!

makes 12 slices (6 servings)

---

1 cup brown sugar
1/2 cup butter or margarine
1 can (29 ounces) sliced peaches, drained
1 Tablespoon vanilla extract
ground cinnamon
12 slices day-old French bread, cut 3/4 inch thick
2 Tablespoons water
5 eggs
1 1/2 cups milk

1 medium saucepan
1 medium mixing bowl
1- 9 x 13 x 2 inch baking dish
Baking Time: 45-50 minutes total
Baking Temperature: 350°

In a saucepan, bring brown sugar, butter and water to a boil; simmer for 10 minutes, stirring frequently.

Pour into a greased 9 x 13 x 2-inch baking dish. Top with peaches. Arrange bread over peaches.

In a medium mixing bowl, whisk the eggs, milk and vanilla. Slowly pour the mixture over the bread. Cover and refrigerate for eight hours or overnight.

Preheat oven to 350°. Remove baking dish from refrigerator and sprinkle with cinnamon. Cover and bake for 20 minutes; remove cover and bake for 25-30 minutes or until golden brown.

Cinnamon Stick Farm
Bed & Breakfast

12364 North Genesee Road
Clio, MI 48420
(810)686-8391
www.cinnamonstickfarmbnb.com
cinstick@tir.com

Hosts: Brian & Carol Powell

Four-time winner of the prestigious "Hospitality Award," the Cinnamon Stick Farm Bed & Breakfast is a large country farm home on 50 rolling acres. There are five guest rooms (one with a Jacuzzi) and many activities to choose from, including walking trails, fishing pond and Belgian draft horses for wagon/sleigh rides. Cinnamon Stick Farm is only minutes from Outlets at Birch Run, Flint and Chesaning. Frankenmuth is 15 miles away.

Rates at Cinnamon Stick Farm range from $60-$130.
Rates include a full breakfast.

Cinnamon Cranberry Muffins

Our guests rave about these muffins, served with our full country breakfast. This easy-to-make recipe will become one of your favorite recipes, too!

makes 12 muffins

---

1 1/2 cups brown sugar
1 1/2 cups flour
1 teaspoon baking soda
1 1/2 teaspoons cinnamon
1/2 teaspoon ground cloves
3/4 cup sour cream
1 egg
1 Tablespoon melted butter
3/4 cup whole berry cranberry sauce

1 medium mixing bowl
1 wooden spoon
1 flour sifter
1 regular sized muffin pan
Baking Time: 1 hour
Baking Temperature: 350°

Preheat oven to 350°. Sift together dry ingredients in a medium mixing bowl. Blend in sour cream, egg, butter and cranberries.

Pour into greased and floured muffin cups; fill about 2/3 full. Sugar can be sprinkled on top before baking or after.

Bake at 350° for 1 hour.

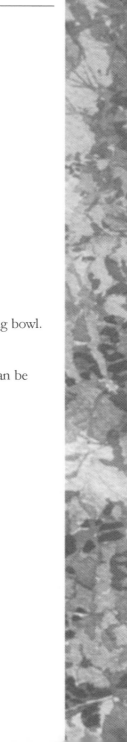

East Tawas Junction
Bed & Breakfast

514 West Bay Street (US 23)
East Tawas, MI 48730
(989)362-8006
www.east-tawas.com
info@east-tawas.com

Hosts: Leigh and Don Mott

Enjoy the Sunrise Side of Northeastern Michigan and sample the turn-of-the-century charm of the East Tawas Junction Bed & Breakfast. This welcoming country Victorian is nestled in a picturesque park-like setting overlooking beautiful Tawas Bay. Five bedrooms, with private baths and cable TV, are decorated and furnished with your comfort in mind.

The parlor's fireplace, piano and VCR encourage pleasant conversations, while the cozy library, cheerful glassed-in porch, sunny decks and garden settings all vie for your attention. After a sumptuous breakfast, skip over to the sugar sand beach or walk, bike or jog to the shops and harbor. Golfing, canoeing, festivals, antiques, concerts, art shows and street dances await you here on the Sunrise Side!

Rates at East Tawas Junction range from $89-$149.
Rates include a full breakfast.

Wowem Waffles with Tangy Cherry Sauce

This recipe calls for ingredients that are easily kept on hand for those weekday guests who just drop in, hoping to find a room available; your weekly shopping schedule is tomorrow! This dish can be prepared quickly and with great flair. Make it special with a side of bacon, ham or sausages (I keep partially cooked bacon and sausages in my freezer for such emergencies). Your guests will wonder how you knew they were coming!

serves 4

Waffles:
2 cups all-purpose flour
1 1/2 cups milk
2/3 cup vinegar
1/3 cup salad oil
2 eggs
1/2 cup dried cherries and/or chopped nuts (optional)

2 medium mixing bowls
1 large pitcher
1 waffle iron

In a medium mixing bowl, mix flour, baking powder, baking soda and salt. Set aside.
In a second medium mixing bowl, whisk eggs; add milk, vinegar and salad oil. Stir flour mixture into milk mixture in 1/2 cup portions until smooth. (Adjust consistency of batter with milk or flour as needed). Add cherries and nuts if desired. Transfer batter into a large pitcher for easy pouring.
Bake in waffle iron as per manufacturer's instructions.

Tangy Cherry Sauce:
1 can (20 ounces) Red Ruby Cherry Pie filling
1/2 cup honey
1/4 cup butter or margarine
1 teaspoon salt
1 teaspoon almond flavoring
1 slice or end of a lemon
dash of cinnamon or nutmeg (optional)

2-quart saucepan

In a 2-quart saucepan, combine ingredients; bring to a boil. Simmer uncovered for a few minutes.

Garnsihes (Choose From):
Whipped cream, powdered sugar, parsley (parsley keeps for weeks if wrapped in dampened paper towel and placed in plastic bag in refrigerator), or available fruits.

To Serve:
Prepare individual plates with a sprig of parsley and any available canned or fresh fruit. Place waffle on each plate, sprinkle with powdered sugar or dollop with a large spoon of whipped cream and top with a spoonful of cherry topping. Serve pitcher of cherry sauce on the side.

Voila! Yet another Bed & Breakfast Speciale!

Josephina's Biscotti

Having fallen in love with Italy after a "if it's Tuesday, it's Belgium" whirlwind trip, subsequently living in the Tuscany region for a year and having the opportunity to travel throughout Italy, I learned much about what makes the Italian cuisine so very special. First and foremost, fresh ingredients purchased daily at the "piazza del mercato." Secondly, a lifestyle that evolves around family, friends and the sharing of a leisurely meal, lovingly prepared and served with an appropriate wine and plenty of water. There is a noticeable lack of pretense, a simplicity and honesty about relationships. Needless to say, "mia cuore e Italia."

Biscotti is a type of Italian cookie that is less sweet than the American treat. They are served at any time but are especially nice at the morning meal. I try to make them available every morning at the coffee bar for those early risers who enjoy a little something to munch on before breakfast is served. This simple recipe is most elegant and was taught to me with much joy by an elderly Italian "amica" who was delighted with my interest in everything Italian. There are many different shapes and forms of biscotti. This was Josephina's favorite.

makes 5 dozen

---

4 cups flour
3 eggs
1 cup lard or vegetable shortening
1 cup sugar
1 teaspoon salt
1 Tablespoon baking powder
1/4 cup milk
2 teaspoons vanilla
cinnamon sugar (optional)

1 large mixing bowl
1 cookie sheet
Baking Time: 8-10 minutes
Baking Temperature: 350°

Preheat oven to 350°. Place flour in a large mixing bowl, adding salt and baking powder. Mix well. Cut lard (or vegetable shortening) into flour mixture until pea size balls appear. Add sugar and eggs. Blend thoroughly. Add enough milk to make a heavy dough. Break the dough into 4 equal balls.

Taking one ball of dough at a time, form into a rectangular roll and place on a floured board. Roll the dough by hand until you have achieved a long pencil-shaped string approximately 3 inches in diameter. You may roll the dough in cinnamon sugar at this time, if you desire. Cut with sharp, floured knife into 3 1/2-inch pieces, shape each piece into an "s" shape and place about 2 inches apart on a greased cookie sheet. Bake at 350 ° for 8-10 minutes. Cool on a wire rack and enjoy, joy, joy.

Another great recipe from East Tawas Junction B&B...

Brunch Enchiladas

Here's a recipe you can count on as a "no fail." Inspired by a trip through the Southwest and New Orleans, it never fails to elicit oohs and aahs! And how we all appreciate those dishes that can be simply put together the evening before the event.

makes 8 servings

2 cups (12 ounces) fully cooked ham, ground
1/2 cup sliced green onions
1/2 cup chopped green pepper
2 1/2 cups shredded Sharp Cheddar cheese (or Mexican Blend)
8 7-inch tortillas
4 eggs, beaten
2 cups light cream or milk
1 Tablespoon all purpose flour
1/4 teaspoon salt
1/4 teaspoon garlic powder
1/4 teaspoon soul seasoning
few drops bottled hot pepper sauce

2 medium mixing bowls
1- 7 x 12 x 2-inch baking dish
Baking Time: 45-50 minutes
Baking Temperature: 350°

In a medium mixing bowl, combine ground ham, onion and green pepper. Place 1/2 cup of the mixture and 3 Tablespoons shredded cheese on one end of each tortilla; roll up. Arrange tortillas, seam side down, in a greased baking dish. Combine eggs, cream, flour, salt, garlic powder, seasoning and hot pepper sauce; pour over tortillas. Cover and refrigerate several hours or overnight.

Preheat oven to 350°. Bake uncovered for 45-50 minutes or until set. Sprinkle with remaining cheese; bake 3 minutes more or until cheese is melted. Let stand 10 minutes before serving.

Cairn House
Bed & Breakfast

8160 Cairn Highway
P.O. Box 858
Elk Rapids, MI 49629
(231)264-8994
www.cairnhouse.com
hperez@cairnhouse.com

Host: Helen Perez

Cairn House Bed & Breakfast is a stately, two-story colonial home in a serene, natural setting located two miles north of the village of Elk Rapids, near Traverse City. Guests are invited to stroll about the one and one-half acres of manicured grounds or view Elk Lake from our porch. Your hostess takes great pleasure in sharing the elegant furnishings collected while living abroad. Relax in front of the fireplace in the spacious living room or retreat to the sun room to enjoy a book.

The "pineapple," the colonial symbol of hospitality, dates back to the days when sea captains returned from their long voyages. Placing a pineapple outside their door signified that they were welcoming friends and neighbors for a visit and sharing their hospitality. Cairn House welcomes you to share warm hospitality while you explore the endless activities available in and around Elk Rapids (near Traverse City).

Rates at Cairn House range from $80-$135.
Rates include a full breakfast.

Scrambled Egg Pillows

This unique recipe is as fun to look at as it is to make! This recipe is great for those times when unexpected company drops by, and you have little time to prepare a delicious breakfast. Your guests and family will ask for it again and again!

serves 4

---

1 package (8 ounces) crescent roll dough
8 large eggs
3 Tablespoons unsalted butter
2 Tablespoons finely chopped chives
1/2 pound ground sausage or turkey sausage, cooked
1/2 pound goat cheese
salt and pepper
dash of milk (optional)
sprigs of chives
fresh grapes, a sprig of mint, orange slices (optional for garnish)

1 medium mixing bowl
1 large frying pan
1 muffin or popover tin
Baking Time: 8-10 minutes
Baking Temperature: 450°

Preheat oven to 450°. Remove and gently roll out crescent roll dough. Instead of tearing into triangles, separate dough by keeping two triangles together, forming a rectangle. Using an ungreased muffin or popover tin, place a rectangle of dough into each muffin cup. Place a second layer of dough over the first layer, placing the second layer perpendicular to the first, to form a small crisscross cup. The cup should resemble an empty pillowcase. Bake for 8-10 minutes. Remove from oven and cool for approximately 5 minutes.

Lightly beat eggs in a medium mixing bowl. If you prefer moist scrambled eggs, add a dash of milk. In a large frying pan, melt butter over medium heat. Add eggs, chives, salt and pepper. Mix well. When eggs are almost ready, add cooked sausage. Stir. Add cheese and stir. Remove from heat.

Pop dough cups from tins and place each one on a plate. Fill the "pillowcases." Spoon egg mixture into cups and garnish with a few sprigs of chives. If desired, garnish plate with fresh grapes, a sprig of mint and orange slices.

The House on the Hill
Bed & Breakfast

9661 Lake Street
Ellsworth, MI 49729
(231) 588-6304
www.thehouseonthehill.com
innkeeper@thehouseonthehill.com

Hosts: Cindy and Tom Tomalka

Imagine an inn on 53 acres of pristine woodlands with a life-size outdoor checkerboard, on-premise hiking and snowshoeing, an evening social hour with complimentary wine, lake frontage with kayaks and a canoe, two of Michigan's finest restaurants within walking distance, renowned breakfasts, friendly guests and hosts, and guest-oriented attention to detail. This isn't your imagination! It is all real at the House on the Hill Bed & Breakfast Inn in Ellsworth.

Rates at the House on the Hill range from $150-$175.
Rates include a full breakfast.

Four-Pepper Frittata

Frittata is an Italian word that translates to "open-faced omelet." This wonderful frittata will cause you to approach the meal with an open mouth! Simple and colorful, this dish will please any guest or family member.

serves 6

2 Tablespoons butter
1/2 red pepper, cut in 1-inch strips
1/2 green pepper, cut in 1-inch strips
1/2 yellow pepper, cut in 1-inch strips
1/2 orange pepper, cut in 1-inch strips
2 cloves garlic, minced
1 Tablespoon fresh dill, chopped
2 cups shredded Asiago cheese
5 large eggs
1 cup half-and-half
1 teaspoon caraway seeds

1- 2 cup mixing bowl
1- 12-inch skillet
1- 9-inch glass pie pan
Baking Time: 30 minutes
Baking Temperature: 350°

Melt butter in 12-inch skillet. Add garlic and cook until fragrant (about 4 minutes). Add peppers and heat through (about 5 minutes). Add chopped dill and toss.

Place pepper mixture in greased 9-inch pie pan. Cover with cheese. Whisk together half-and-half and eggs. Pour over peppers. Sprinkle caraway seeds over frittata. Bake as instructed; use edge protectors to avoid burning, if necessary.

The Kingsley House
Bed & Breakfast

626 West Main Street
Fennville, MI 49408
(269)561-6425
www.kingsleyhouse.com
garyking@accn.org

Hosts: Gary and Kari King

"Elegant Victorian" best describes this Queen Anne style turreted mansion. Built in 1886, the Kingsley House boasts eight guest rooms, each with private baths and some with Jacuzzis and fireplaces. All of the rooms are named after apples in honor of the home's builder, Harvey Kingsley, who introduced apple trees to this area of Michigan over 100 years ago.

The inn is located just minutes from Saugatuck, Holland and Lake Michigan beaches. In summer, enjoy golfing, shopping and water sports of all kinds. In winter, we are just steps from cross country skiing and ice skating. Come relax with us!

Rates at the Kingsley House range from $85-$175.
Rates include a full breakfast.

Apple Bread

This recipe helped a friend get her Girl Scout cooking badge over 60 years ago! We always use local apples from our nearby orchards.

makes 1 loaf

1/2 cup shortening
1 cup sugar
2 eggs
1 teaspoon baking soda
2 Tablespoons sour milk
2 cups flour
1 teaspoon vanilla
2 cups apples, peeled and chopped

Topping:
2 Tablespoons butter
2 Tablespoons flour
1 teaspoon cinnamon

1 large mixing bowl
1 small mixing bowl
1 loaf pan
Baking Time: 1 hour
Baking Temperature: 350°

Preheat oven to 350°. In a large mixing bowl, mix all ingredients in the order given. Add topping. Bake in greased loaf pan for 1 hour.

Topping:
In a small mixing bowl, mix all ingredients with a pastry blender until mixture resembles coarse crumbs. Sprinkle on top of apple bread *before* baking.

Another great recipe from the Kingsley House......

Baked Apple French Toast

This recipe is prepared the night before, then refrigerated and baked in the morning. We use local apples from our nearby orchards!

serves 9 (one-slice servings)

---

1 cup packed brown sugar
1/2 cup (1 stick) margarine
2 Tablespoons light corn syrup
2 large tart apples (such as Granny Smith), peeled and sliced 1/4 inch thick
3 eggs
1 cup milk
1 teaspoon vanilla
9 slices day old French bread, sliced 3/4 inch thick

Apple Syrup:
1 cup sugar
1 1/2 cups apple cider or apple juice
2 1/2 Tablespoons cornstarch
1 teaspoon cinnamon
1/2 teaspoon nutmeg

1 small saucepan
1 medium saucepan
1- 9 x 13 x 2-inch pan
Baking Time: 35-40 minutes
Baking Temperature: 350°

In a small saucepan, cook margarine, brown sugar and corn syrup until thick (medium heat works best). Pour into ungreased pan. Arrange apple slices on top. Beat eggs, milk and vanilla together. Dip bread slices into egg mixture. Place bread over apples. Cover and refrigerate overnight. Remove from refrigerator 30 minutes before baking.

Preheat oven to 350°. Bake uncovered for 35-40 minutes. Serve with apple syrup.

Apple Syrup:
In a medium saucepan, combine all ingredients in order given. Place the pan over medium heat and cook, stirring constantly until the mixture comes to a boil. Stir while boiling for 1 minute. Keep syrup warm. Serve with apple French toast. Keep leftover syrup in refrigerator; it can be reheated. Keeps for about one week.

Another great recipe from the Kingsley House......

Kingsley Breakfast Potatoes

These breakfast potatoes are a wonderful change from everyday hash browns. They are a nice accompaniment to eggs or quiche. Add more Mrs. Dash for a "spicy" taste!

serves 6

6 medium potatoes, peeled and cut in half lengthwise
1 Tablespoon dried minced onion
1 teaspoon Mrs. Dash seasoning-original flavor
1 1/2 Tablespoons vegetable oil

1 large plastic food storage bag
1 large frying pan

Place potatoes in a large plastic food storage bag and cook on high for 6 minutes in the microwave. Let cool.

Place vegetable oil in a large frying pan. Cube potatoes and place in pan.

Add minced onion and Mrs. Dash.

Fry until very lightly browned over medium high heat.

Bavarian Town Bed & Breakfast

206 Beyerlein Street
Frankenmuth, MI 48734
(989) 652-8057
www.laketolake.com/bavarian
btbedb@juno.com

Hosts: Louie and Kathy Weiss

Open since 1985, the Bavarian Town Bed & Breakfast is a beautifully decorated, smoke-free Cape Cod home. The home is located in a quiet residential neighborhood, and the bedrooms are decorated in college motifs. Guests are welcomed to the bed & breakfast with a hospitality hour, where the hosts share recipes and information on the area. Each bedroom has a king bed, television and private toilet and sink. The shower is shared. Guests are invited to enjoy the hot tub on the deck and the sauna in the basement. Your hosts are fluent in German and English. Credit cards are accepted. Great shopping and well-known restaurants are a short distance from the Bavarian Town Bed & Breakfast.

Rates at Bavarian Town range from $80-$100.
Rates include a full breakfast.

Bavarian Egg Dish

This recipe is one of our favorites as it can be individualized for each guest. We ask what ingredients each guest likes or does not like and make the individual dishes accordingly. Some guests prefer one egg while others want two. Others might like to substitute egg beaters for regular eggs. Some might like chopped onions with it, also. It is easy to make for up to 6 or 8 guests. We serve it with homemade bread and homemade jams and jellies from our kitchen.

serves 6-8

1/2 pound medium sliced ham, enough to cover bottom of dishes
1 can (4.5 ounces) sliced mushrooms (2 Tablespoons for each dish)
1 package fresh or frozen broccoli or asparagus, cooked
6-16 eggs (1 or 2 eggs for each dish—egg beaters may be substituted)
1 1/2 – 2 cups Baby Swiss cheese, grated (1/4 cup for each dish)
1 1/2 – 2 cups three-cheese combination, grated (1/4 cup for each dish)
6-8 Tablespoons milk (1Tablespoon for each dish)
6-8 teaspoons parsley, shredded (1 teaspoon for each dish)

Chopped onions, optional

6-8 individual 5-6 inch oval or round ovenware dishes
Baking Time: 15-20 minutes
Baking Temperature: 350°

Spray bottoms and sides of ovenware dishes with nonstick cooking spray. Layer bottoms of dishes with ham slices. Add sliced mushrooms. Thinly spread slightly pre-cooked broccoli or asparagus. Add onions, if desired. Add one or two eggs to each dish. Do not scramble the eggs. Cover with Baby Swiss cheese and three-cheese combination. Add milk and parsley.

Bake at 350° for 15-20 minutes until set. Serve in baking dishes.

The Kipling House Bed & Breakfast

1716 North Lakeshore Drive
Gladstone, MI 49837
(877)905-ROOM(7666)
www.kiplinghouse.com
info@kiplinghouse.com

Hosts: Ann and Ralph Miller

"Welcome to the Kipling House," located in the heart of Michigan's beautiful Upper Peninsula. This 1897 boarding house has been lovingly restored to reflect yesterday's charm and today's elegance and convenience.

Filled with community history, the Kipling House has been recognized as one of the finest restoration projects in the area. Ann and Ralph specialize in great food, good conversation and lasting memories. Open year round, visitors enjoy the garden or gazebo in the summer and curling up with a book and a cup of tea by the fireplace in the winter.

The "Garden Cottage" is a highlight with guests, especially cross-country skiers and anniversary couples. This cottage is set aside from the main house, overlooking the water garden.

The U.P. offers thousands of acres of forests and streams for the outdoor enthusiast who wants a "get back to nature" experience.

Rates at the Kipling House range from $75-$150.
Rates include a full breakfast and dessert in the evening.

Cinnamon Swirl French Toast
Served with Caramel Banana Rum Sauce

This is only one of Ralph's many culinary delights. The cinnamon swirl bread can be ordered through a food distributor like Sysco. The caramel banana rum sauce is wonderful, or you can use the syrup of your choice. Our guests love this breakfast, or it makes a wonderful dessert with ice cream.

serves 4

---

8 slices of round cinnamon swirl bread
1 cup strongly brewed coffee
1/4 cup hazelnut creamer
6 eggs
2 cups corn flakes, crushed

Sauce:
1 stick margarine
1 cup brown sugar
1/2 cup heavy cream
1 shot good rum
2 bananas, sliced

whipped cream, optional

1 medium mixing bowl
1 saucepan
1 skillet
1 baking sheet
Baking Time: 10 minutes
Baking Temperature: 350°

Whip eggs, coffee and creamer in medium mixing bowl. Dip bread in mixture, soaking completely. Cover each slice with crushed corn flakes and brown both sides in a skillet.

Place on baking sheet and bake for 10 minutes at 350°.

Sauce:
Melt margarine and brown sugar in saucepan until bubbly. Remove from heat and slowly whisk in cream and rum.

Add sliced bananas to mixture just before serving. Garnish with whipped cream, if desired, and enjoy.

Another great recipe from The Kipling House...

Seafood Quiche

This is a wonderful, easy dish that you can make the night before and warm in the morning. We serve this quiche with toasted crumpets and pear and walnut muffins with almond frosting. You can substitute crumbled cooked bacon and onions for the seafood and a teaspoon of nutmeg instead of Old Bay Seasoning.

serves 6

---

4 eggs
2 cups half-and-half
1/2 cup Bisquick
1 teaspoon Old Bay Seasoning
1 teaspoon parsley
salt and pepper
1 cup grated Swiss cheese
1 cup finely chopped crabmeat (imitation crabmeat can be substituted)

Herb Sauce:
3 ounces cream cheese
4 Tablespoons butter
1/2 teaspoon Old Bay Seasoning
1/2 cup half-and-half

1 medium mixing bowl
1 blender
1 9-inch pie plate
1 medium saucepan
Baking Time: 1 hour
Baking Temperature: 350°

Preheat oven to 350°. Blend eggs, half-and-half, Bisquick, seasoning, parsley and salt and pepper thoroughly in a blender. Spray a 9-inch pie plate with nonstick cooking spray. Place Swiss cheese in bottom of plate. Add crabmeat. Pour egg mixture over meat and cheese.

Bake for 1 hour at 350°.

Herb Sauce:
Combine all ingredients in a medium saucepan. Stir over low heat until blended. Serve warm with quiche.

Another great recipe from The Kipling House...

Peaches in a Cloud

This warm and wonderful breakfast is one of our guests' favorites. Good enough to "melt in your mouth." You can use either fresh or canned peaches. The Kipling House serves it with sausage on the side.

serves 2

Puffy Omelet:
4 eggs, separated
1/4 teaspoon cream of tartar
1/4 teaspoon salt
1/4 cup cold water
1 Tablespoon powdered sugar
2 Tablespoons butter

Peach Sauce:
1 large can (29 ounces) sliced peaches, drained, reserving juice
1/4 cup sugar
1 Tablespoon cornstarch

1 small mixing bowl
1 large mixing bowl
1 mixer
1 oven-safe 10-inch skillet
1 small saucepan
Baking Time: 10 minutes
Baking Temperature: 350°

Puffy Omelet:
Preheat oven to 350°. In a large mixing bowl, beat egg whites until foamy. Add cream of tartar. Beat until stiff peaks form. In a small mixing bowl, beat egg yolks, salt, sugar and water until light and fluffy. Carefully fold into beaten egg whites. Melt butter in oven-safe 10-inch skillet over medium heat. Add egg mixture and cook for 3 minutes. Place skillet in 350° oven and bake for 10 minutes. Omelet is done when it is golden brown and springs back when touched.

Peach Sauce:
Set peaches aside and heat juice with sugar and cornstarch until thick and bubbly. Add sliced peaches to liquid.

Cut egg omelet in half and carefully separate. Fill center with peach sauce. Assemble on a plate and sprinkle with powdered sugar.

The State Street Inn

646 State Street
Harbor Beach, MI 48441
(989)479-3388
www.thestatestreetinn.com
info@thestatestreetinn.com

Hosts: Bill and Janice Duerr

Welcome to our century old country Victorian Bed & Breakfast in a quaint lakeside community on Lake Huron in Michigan's thumb. Guests enjoy old fashioned hospitality and find the quiet, cozy and romantic atmosphere reminiscent of an earlier era. Three unique and inviting guest rooms await you and promise a warm and memorable stay. All guest rooms have a private bath, cable television, VCR and air conditioning.

Within a short walking distance, guests will find parks, marinas, fishing, golf, swimming, shopping, antiques, lighthouses and much more. After a day exploring the area, guests return for an evening snack while they relax in the parlor, library or the veranda overlooking the gardens.

Rates at the State Street Inn range from $65-$85.
Rates include a full breakfast and evening dessert.

Coconut Blueberry Muffins

These muffins smell great — kind of like a coconut macaroon. They are not overly sweet, they are easy to make and are wonderful served warm. We serve these muffins for breakfast with fresh fruit and our famous egg casserole.

makes 1 dozen muffins

---

1 1/2 cups white flour
3/4 cup granulated sugar
1/2 cup shredded coconut
1/2 teaspoon salt
1 teaspoon cinnamon
1 Tablespoon baking powder
1 stick butter, melted
1 Tablespoon vanilla extract
1 egg
1/2 cup cream or half-and-half
1 cup fresh or frozen blueberries — if frozen, keep in freezer until ready to stir
      into batter.

1 small mixing bowl
1 large mixing bowl
1 muffin pan — 12 count
Baking Time: 20-25 minutes
Baking Temperature: 350°

Combine all dry ingredients, including coconut, in a large mixing bowl and stir well with spoon to thoroughly blend. Melt butter in microwave safe dish, about 30 seconds. In a small mixing bowl, mix cream, vanilla and egg. Add melted butter to wet ingredients and combine.

Pour all wet ingredients into dry ingredients and mix well to blend. Add blueberries to batter and blend gently. Batter is quite thick. Drop by the spoonful into muffin papers in muffin pan and fill about 3/4 full. Bake in 350° oven for 20-25 minutes or until golden brown.

Adrounie House
Bed & Breakfast

126 South Broadway
Hastings, MI 49058
(800)927-8505
www.adrounie.com

Hosts: April and Don Tubbs

This 1894 Queen Ann Michigan Historical Site has been lovingly restored to reflect the Victorian era with lots of antiques and collectibles throughout. The six guest rooms, all tastefully decorated with their own personality, include private baths, televisions and air conditioning. Our guests enjoy the relaxed, peaceful atmosphere and comfy beds with freshly ironed sheets. We are within walking distance to shopping, antiques, restaurants and a four screen theater.

Rates at the Adrounie House range from $65-$125.
Rates include a full breakfast.

Pumpkin Sour Cream Pancakes

This light and airy breakfast treat is a fall favorite. Mixing the dry ingredients the night before gives a quick start to the preparation. Often, our corporate guests require different serving times, and this flavorful pancake served with sausage and fresh fruit is a hit with guests and innkeepers.

makes 6-7 five-inch pancakes or 12 three-inch pancakes

1 cup all-purpose flour
1 Tablespoon baking powder
1/4 teaspoon salt
1/4 teaspoon cinnamon
1/8 teaspoon nutmeg
2 Tablespoons sugar
1 egg
1 cup buttermilk
1/4 cup sour cream
1/4 cup canned pumpkin
1 Tablespoon butter, melted
1 Tablespoon vanilla
powdered sugar

1 small mixing bowl
1 medium mixing bowl
1 griddle

Mix flour, baking powder, salt, spices and sugar together in a medium mixing bowl. Combine remaining ingredients in a small mixing bowl. Slowly whisk liquids into dry ingredients.

Cook pancakes on preheated griddle that has been brushed with butter. (Olive oil or cooking oil can be used instead of butter.) Pour approximately 1/3 cup of batter per pancake onto griddle and cook over medium heat. When bubbles appear on top, turn over and cook for a few minutes on the other side. Do not overcook; the pancakes should be moist.

Sprinkle a dusting of powdered sugar over the pancakes before serving.

Serve hot with butter and warm maple syrup.

Another great recipe from the Adrounie House....

Flourless Peanut Butter Cookies

These cookies get raves from our guests and lots of requests for the recipe. They are great for the health conscious people who are trying to avoid white flour. Trying to keep them in the guest cookie jar and away from my husband is the challenge.

makes 9 dozen cookies

---

1 1/2 cups peanut butter
1/2 cup butter, softened
1 cup sugar
1 cup packed brown sugar
3 eggs
1 teaspoon vanilla extract
4 1/2 cups old fashioned oats
2 teaspoons baking soda
1 cup semi-sweet chocolate chips
1 cup dried cranberries or dried cherries
1 cup chopped walnuts

2 large mixing bowls
2 baking sheets
Baking Time: 12-14 minutes
Baking Temperature: 350°

Preheat oven to 350°. In a large mixing bowl, cream peanut butter, butter and sugars. Add eggs one at a time, beating well after each addition. Beat in vanilla. In another large mixing bowl, combine oats and baking soda. Gradually add this mixture to the creamed mixture. Stir in chips, cranberries or cherries and walnuts.

Drop by heaping Tablespoonsful 2 inches apart onto ungreased baking sheets. Bake at 350° for 12-14 minutes or until edges of cookies are browned. Remove to wire racks to cool.

Another great recipe from the Adrounie House....

Blueberry Stuffed French Toast

This yummy dish is a guest favorite that we serve all year round. The great thing about this recipe is that it can be cut down to 4 servings by cutting all ingredients in half and baking in a 9 x 9 inch glass dish. We serve this with bacon or sausage and a fresh fruit cup.

serves 8 or 9

---

12 slices "Texas Toast" bread, crusts removed and cubed
1 1/2 packages (8 ounces each) cream cheese, cubed
1 cup fresh or frozen blueberries
12 eggs
1/3 cup maple syrup
1/4 teaspoon nutmeg
2 cups milk

Topping:
1 cup orange juice or water
1 cup granulated sugar
1/4 teaspoon nutmeg
2 Tablespoons cornstarch
2 cups fresh or frozen blueberries
1 Tablespoon butter, melted
1 Tablespoon lemon juice

1 large mixing bowl
1 small saucepan
1- 9 x 13 inch glass baking dish (will serve 8) or 1 12 x 10 inch baking dish (will serve 9)
Baking Time: 1 hour total
Baking Temperature: 325°

Spray 9 x 13 inch glass baking dish with nonstick cooking spray and place half of the bread cubes in the bottom. Evenly place the cream cheese cubes over the bread and scatter blueberries over the cream cheese. Place the remaining bread cubes over the blueberries. In a large mixing bowl, beat together eggs, syrup, milk and nutmeg. Pour the egg mixture over the bread and cheese. Cover with plastic wrap and chill overnight. Preheat oven to 325°. Remove plastic wrap and cover with aluminum foil. Bake for 30 minutes, then remove aluminum foil. Bake for 30 minutes more.

Cut the French toast into serving pieces. Pour warm sauce over each piece and serve immediately.

Topping:
In a small saucepan, combine the orange juice, sugar, nutmeg and cornstarch. Stir until mixed. Add the blueberries and cook until the sauce thickens, stirring frequently. Mix in the melted butter and lemon juice.

Keep warm. Pour over the French toast.

The Inn
at Old Orchard Road

1422 South Shore Drive
Holland, MI 49423
(616)335-2525
www.laketolake.com
orchardroad@chartermi.net

Host: Elizabeth DeWaard

Revel in fresh lake breezes or fluffy, lake-effect snow at this big old 1906 Dutch farmhouse filled with antiques. Three cozy rooms, all with private baths, await your presence during any of the four beautiful seasons in Holland. A full breakfast will prepare you for swimming, hiking, cross-country skiing, shopping or sightseeing, after which you may wish to relax on the front porch or back patio, or in a big chair with a book. The resident pets will welcome your homecoming with much purring and wagging of tails!

Rates at the Inn at Old Orchard Road range from $85-$95.
Rates include a full breakfast.

Egg-chiladas

This "rib-sticking" recipe can be prepared the night before and is totally gobbled up by the guests! Serve with a hash brown patty, warmed corn relish and some sweet fruit for a hearty start to the day.

serves 6

12- 7-inch flour tortillas
1 1/2 cups cooked ham, cubed, or 8 cooked sausage patties, crumbled
3/4 cup onion, chopped
2 cups Cheddar cheese, shredded, divided
8 eggs
2 1/2 cups milk
1/4 teaspoon salt
1 Tablespoon flour

Toppings:
Sour cream
Mild salsa

1 medium mixing bowl
1 large mixing bowl
1- 9 x 15 x 2-inch glass baking pan
Baking Time: 45 minutes
Baking Temperature: 350°

Preheat oven to 350°. Spray a 9 x 15 x 2-inch glass baking pan with nonstick cooking spray.

In a medium mixing bowl, combine ham or sausage, onions and 1 cup cheese. Spoon 1/4 cup of the mixture down the center of each tortilla. Roll up the tortillas and set in prepared pan seam side down (with two tortillas placed along the edge).

In a large mixing bowl, beat eggs, milk, salt and flour until smooth. Pour mixture over tortillas. Cover with foil and refrigerate for 8 hours or overnight.

Remove from refrigerator 30 minutes before baking. Bake, covered, for 35 minutes. Then uncover and bake for 10 additional minutes. Sprinkle with remaining cheese. Place in the oven until cheese is melted, about 4 minutes.

Let stand for 10 minutes before serving. Garnish with a dollop of sour cream and two Tablespoons of mild salsa.

Strawberry-Almond Muffins

These muffins are "melt-in-your-mouth" rich! Guests love the combination of flavors and the cake-like texture.

makes 6 jumbo muffins

---

1 1/2 cups all purpose flour
1/2 cup sugar
2 teaspoons baking powder
1 egg
1/2 cup whole milk
1/2 cup butter, melted and cooled
1/4 teaspoon almond extract
1 cup sliced strawberries, dry
granulated sugar

1 small mixing bowl
1 large mixing bowl
1 jumbo muffin tin
Baking Time: 22-25 minutes
Baking Temperature: 375°

Preheat oven to 375°. In a large mixing bowl, combine flour, sugar and baking powder.

In a small mixing bowl, beat egg, milk and extract together. Add melted butter.

Pour liquid mixture into dry ingredients and stir until just moistened. Gently fold in strawberries.

Fill greased jumbo muffin cups about 2/3 full. Bake at 375° for 22-25 minutes.

While still warm, sprinkle tops with granulated sugar.

Another great recipe from the Inn at Old Orchard Road...

Frozen Fruit N Cream

This recipe is wonderful any time of the year but especially on Valentine's Day or Christmas. This fruit combination not only tastes terrific but looks great, too!

serves 14

---

8 ounces cream cheese, whipped
2 cups frozen, whipped nondairy topping (do not thaw)
1/2 cup sifted confectioner's sugar
1 cup chopped walnuts
2 cans (1 pound each) cranberry sauce
2 cans (1 pound each) crushed pineapple
14 walnut halves for decoration

1 medium mixing bowl
1 large mixing bowl
1 cookie sheet
14 9-ounce plastic cups

In a medium mixing bowl, beat cream cheese, frozen topping and confectioner's sugar together until smooth. Stir in nuts. Neatly spoon a scant 1/4 cup into the bottoms of the plastic cups.

In a large mixing bowl, combine, cranberry sauce and crushed pineapple; mix well. Add 1/2 cup of mixture to each plastic cup.

Place on a cookie sheet, cover with plastic wrap and freeze. To remove from cup, dip bottom and sides quickly in warm water. Store in freezer bags.

Remove desired quantity from freezer and place on small decorative dishes 1 hour before serving. Press a walnut half in the cream top.

Shaded Oaks
Bed & Breakfast

444 Oak Street
Holland, MI 49424
(616)399-4194
www.shadedoaks.com
shadedoaks@chartermi.net

Hosts: Jack and Karen Zibell

Shaded Oaks Bed & Breakfast is a charming Cape Cod in a wooded setting by Lake Macatawa. Experience simple or extravagant luxury in our beautifully appointed suites with private baths. Start your day with a full breakfast, traditional or gourmet, before you are off to enjoy Lake Michigan activities. We are within walking distance to Holland State Park and bike trails. Don't miss this opportunity to relax and retreat in style.

Rates at Shaded Oaks range from $139-$189.
Rates include a full breakfast.

Caramel Apple Waffles

These delightfully light golden waffles with apples and a butterscotch/caramel topping are sure to bring smiles and kudos at the breakfast table. Serve with 2 sausage patties and your favorite fruit garnish on the plate.

serves 4 (2 squares per person using a Belgian-type waffle iron)

Waffles:
4 eggs, separated
1 cup milk
1 cup buttermilk or half-and-half.
1 stick butter, melted
1 teaspoon vanilla plus a little more
1 small drizzle honey
1/2 teaspoon maple syrup
1 teaspoon baking soda
1 teaspoon baking powder
1/2 teaspoon salt
3 Tablespoons sugar
1 3/4 cups flour

Caramel Sauce:
6 Tablespoons butter, melted
2 apples, peeled and sliced (Red Delicious work well)
1/3 cup butterscotch caramel topping (Sanders dessert topping—butterscotch caramel—is the
          best we've found)
1 teaspoon brown sugar
1 Tablespoon maple syrup

1 small mixing bowl
1 large mixing bowl
1 saucepan
1 waffle iron

Waffles:
In a large mixing bowl, mix the dry ingredients and whisk together. Heat the milk to slightly warm to the touch (don't heat the buttermilk). Melt the butter; don't scald and let cool for a few minutes after melted. Whip the egg whites until just whipped – don't overwhip or the waffles get tough. Err on the side of underwhipping—this is important!

The order the ingredients are added is critical. I have no idea why, but it changes the way they come out. Add ingredients in the following order: egg yolks, milk…don't pour it all in. Depending on the size of the egg, you may not need it at all. Add butter, honey, syrup and vanilla. Mix these ingredients with an egg beater.

Very gently mix in the whisked dry ingredients until they are wet; overmixing will result in tough waffles. Pour the egg whites on top and with a very large spoon, fold the wet batter on top of the egg whites. Don't mix; just slightly fold in.

This recipe turns out best if made very late the evening before. Cover it and put the bowl in another larger bowl with a little ice around it so things don't spoil. Ideally, it should be exactly at room temperature when you pour it in the waffle iron. Be careful; the eggs and milk may spoil if left out too long.

Caramel Sauce:
In a saucepan, add apples to the melted butter. Cook until slightly soft. Add butterscotch topping, brown sugar and maple syrup in the order given. Stir until completely heated.

Spoon over finished waffles—serve and enjoy the compliments you will surely get!

The Thistle Inn

300 North 152nd Avenue
Holland, MI 49424
(616)399-0409
www.web.triton.net/p/patteske
patteske@Triton.net

Hosts: Gary and Pat Teske

The Thistle Inn is located on the north side of Holland, close to Lake Michigan and right on a bike path. The area is best known for its annual Tulip Time Festival but is wonderful year round. The inn's guest rooms feature private baths, air conditioning, television, in-room coffee, tea and soft drinks, and each room opens to a patio with a large hot tub in a lovely private outdoor setting.

Rates at the Thistle Inn range from $90-$110.
Rates include a full breakfast.

Stuffed Apricot French Toast

This is a delicious and very easy recipe to prepare and serve. It can be altered to serve 1,2, 6 or any number of guests. Most of it can be done the night before by slicing and filling the bread, then refrigerating it in a Ziplock bag.

serves 6-8

1 loaf (16 ounces) French bread, unsliced
1 or 1 1/2 packages (8 ounces each) honey nut cream cheese
4 eggs
3/4 cup half-and-half
1/2 teaspoon nutmeg
1/2 teaspoon vanilla

Topping:
1 jar (12 ounces) apricot jam
1 cup orange juice
1 Tablespoon cornstarch

1 small to medium mixing bowl
1 small to medium saucepan
1 cookie sheet
1 griddle or electric frying pan
Baking Time: 20 minutes
Baking Temperature: 300°

Cut the French bread into 1 1/2 to 2-inch slices. Cut a pocket in the top of each slice and fill with 1 1/2 to 2 Tablespoons of honey nut cream cheese.

Beat eggs, half-and-half and nutmeg in a bowl and dip both sides of the bread in the mixture. Cook on lightly greased griddle until golden brown on both sides. Place on ungreased cookie sheet in a 300° oven for 20 minutes. Place 1 or 2 slices on each guest's plate, cover with topping and serve.

Topping:
Combine apricot jam with half of the orange juice in a small to medium saucepan. Mix the cornstarch in the remaining orange juice and add this to the mixture in the saucepan.

Heat until thickened while stirring constantly.

Drizzle over each serving of French toast.

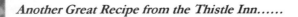

Another Great Recipe from the Thistle Inn......

Frozen Fruit Cup

I received this recipe 20 years ago from a friend, Shirley, in Battle Creek, MI, who was a home economist with the local gas company and did cooking demonstrations. It is extremely easy and wonderful to have on hand.

makes 15-16 cups

---

2 packages (16 ounces) frozen sliced strawberries, thawed
2 cans (6 ounces) or 1 can (12 ounces) frozen orange juice, thawed
2 cans (20 ounces) crushed pineapple
1 can (16 ounces) mandarin oranges-do not drain
1/3 cup lemon juice
5 bananas, sliced

1 large mixing bowl
15-16 paper or plastic cups

Combine all ingredients in a large mixing bowl—do not drain the fruit.

Spoon into paper or plastic cups, such as the 9 ounce "Solo" flexible cups. Freeze until firm. Once frozen, you may package in freezer bags for future use as needed.

I take them from the freezer and place them in the refrigerator the night before I'll be serving them. In the morning, I empty the bags into individual serving dishes. You may want to experiment with the thawing time until you find your preference—some like them quite chilled.

Another Great Recipe from the Thistle Inn......

Blueberry and Peach Crepes

Since Holland is in the center of the largest blueberry producing area in the country, this is a wonderful way to enjoy locally grown fruit. Both the crepes and sauce can be made ahead of time and assembled just before serving. You may also substitute a different fruit filling if you desire.

serves 10 (2 crepes per serving)

Crepes:
1 1/2 cups milk
1 1/4 cups flour
2 Tablespoons sugar
3 eggs
2 Tablespoons butter, melted
dash of salt

Filling:
8-10 ripe peaches
sugar to taste

Sauce:
2 Tablespoons cornstarch
2/3 cup sugar
6 Tablespoons water
2 Tablespoons lemon juice
4 cups blueberries
dash of salt
whipped cream for garnish

2 medium mixing bowls
1 crepe pan or small skillet
1 saucepan

Crepes:
Combine all ingredients in a medium mixing bowl; beat with whisk until well blended and then let sit for 15-30 minutes. Lightly spray a crepe pan or small skillet with nonstick cooking spray. Heat pan, then add about 1/4 cup batter. Tilt pan to spread batter and heat until edges are slightly dry and underside is light brown, about 1 minute. Turn and cook for about 30 seconds more. Invert crepe onto paper towel on rack to cool. Repeat until all of the batter is used. When cool, you may place the crepes, along with the paper towels, in a Ziploc bag. Refrigerate if not using within a day or two.

Filling:
Peel about 8-10 ripe peaches and slice. Place in a bowl and add sugar to taste. Let stand for about 10-20 minutes.

Sauce:
Combine all ingredients in a saucepan and bring to a boil, stirring constantly. Simmer for about 2-3 minutes until sauce appears clear. Makes 3 cups.

To Serve:
Warm crepes between paper towels in microwave for about 20 seconds. Remove paper towels. Spoon peaches down the center of the crepe, roll up and place seam side down on a serving plate. Spoon warm blueberry sauce over crepe and garnish with whipped cream.

Hall House
Bed & Breakfast

106 Thompson Street
Kalamazoo, MI 49006
(616) 343-2500
www.hallhouse.com
thefoxes@hallhouse.com

Hosts: Scott and Terri Fox

Hall House is located in the National Historic District on the edge of the Kalamazoo College campus and within walking distance of Western Michigan University. This 14-room Georgian Revival home was built by prominent contractor Henry L. Vander Horst in 1923 and features mahogany woodwork, pewabic tile entryway, and a hand-painted mural in the library. Hall House has six guest rooms/suites which can accommodate from two to five guests. All rooms have private baths (some with soaking tubs, Jacuzzi, fireplaces, and CD players), cable TV/VCR (w/video library), telephones, bathrobes, and air conditioning. Theater, restaurants, antiques, and golf are nearby, and complimentary refreshments are always available.

Rates at Hall House range from $79-$145.
Rates include a full breakfast on weekends and a continental plus breakfast weekdays.

Breakfast Casserole

This breakfast casserole can be partially prepared the night before and finished in the morning. It's very filling and falls into the comfort food category! Serve with warm whole wheat banana muffins and fresh orange juice.

serves 4-6

---

1 pound bulk sausage, crumbled, or smoked sausage cut into bite size pieces
1 green pepper, diced
1 medium onion, diced
8 ounces sliced mushrooms
2 pounds frozen hash browns
6-8 large eggs
salt & pepper to taste

Crumbled bacon may be substituted for the sausage.

1 sauté pan
1 electric skillet
1 9x13-inch casserole dish
Baking Time: 15-20 minutes
Baking Temperature: 350°

Cook sausage in electric skillet. Remove from skillet and drain grease. Set aside. In same skillet, fry hash browns according to package instructions.

In a sauté pan, sauté green peppers, onions and mushrooms until tender. Combine with sausage and hash browns in an oven-safe, greased casserole dish. These steps may be completed the night before. Cover casserole dish and refrigerate.

Scramble eggs in electric skillet until soft; do not overcook. Combine with other ingredients in casserole dish and place in 350° oven for 15-20 minutes or until warmed through.

Aspen House
Bed & Breakfast

1353 North Manitou Trail
P.O. Box 722
Leland, MI 49654
(231)256-9724
www.aspenhouseleland.com
info@aspenhouseleland.com

Hosts: Phil and Paula Swink

An open door invites you into an atmosphere of country elegance nestled between Lake Leelanau and Lake Michigan. Enjoy the intimate atmosphere of a European Bed & Breakfast in this restored 1880s farmhouse spilling over with Old World charm and comfort…a magical place to curl up and relax after a full day or simply to escape from the daily race.

Rates at Aspen House range from $125-$175.
Rates include a full breakfast.

Portabella Mushroom & Spinach Benedict

This breakfast will challenge your guests' palates with a new version of an old breakfast favorite, eggs benedict. This is a favorite at the Aspen House and returning guests often request it.

serves 6

12 eggs, poached ahead of time and placed in ice water
6 large Portabella mushrooms
2 large garlic cloves, finely chopped
1/2 cup extra virgin olive oil
1 package (6 ounces) fresh washed spinach
3 green onions, chopped
3 Tablespoons butter

Sauce:
1 cup dry white wine
2 Tablespoons rice vinegar
2 Tablespoons shallots, finely chopped
1 cup heavy cream
1/2 cup (1 stick) butter, softened
3 Tablespoons fresh lemon, thyme or tarragon

1 two-quart saucepan
1 broiler pan
1 10 or 12 inch skillet
1 large pan for poaching or egg poacher

Poach 12 eggs 4-5 minutes and plunge them into ice water; set aside.

Preheat broiler. Remove stems from mushrooms. Combine garlic and olive oil and brush both sides of mushrooms well. Broil mushrooms about 3 minutes on each side, remove and keep warm in low oven. Wilt spinach and green onions in butter just until coated and spinach is softened or wilted. Plunge poached eggs in boiling water for 2 minutes to reheat. Place a warm mushroom on each plate. Top with spinach and onion. Place 2 poached eggs on top. Generously spoon sauce over eggs and finish with fresh cracked pepper.

Sauce:
In a two-quart saucepan, combine white wine and shallots and cook to reduce to 2 Tablespoons of liquid. Remove the shallots with a slotted spoon and press out any liquid into the saucepan. Add the heavy cream and herbs to the liquid and reduce again by one third.

Whisk butter into warm mixture over low heat and keep warm until ready to serve.

McGee Homestead
Bed & Breakfast

2534 Alden Nash NE
Lowell, MI 49331
(616)897-8142
www.iserv.net/~mcgeebb
mcgeebb@iserv.net

Hosts: Bill and Ardie Barber

Wake up to the rooster crowing! Our 1880s brick farmhouse is set on five acres surrounded by orchards. There's a big ol' barn filled with animals. The guest area has a living room with fireplace, parlor, small kitchen and big screen porch with hot tub. All rooms have private baths and antiques.

Rates at McGee Homestead range from $52-$72.
Rates include a full country breakfast.

10 Cup Cookies

When you come to our Bed & Breakfast, we want you to feel like you're visiting Grandma. We keep the cookie jar full in the guest kitchen. These cookies are our guests' favorite.

makes 5 dozen cookies

1 cup butter or margarine
1 cup peanut butter
1 cup sugar
1 cup packed brown sugar
2 eggs
1 teaspoon vanilla
1 cup flour
1 teaspoon baking soda
1/2 teaspoon baking powder
1 cup sweetened flaked coconut
1 cup semi-sweet chocolate chips
1 cup raisins or dates
1 cup chopped walnuts
1 cup quick cooking oats

1 large mixing bowl
1 medium mixing bowl
2 or 3 cookie sheets
Baking Time: 12-15 minutes
Baking Temperature: 350°

Preheat oven to 350°. In a large mixing bowl, cream butter, peanut butter, sugar, brown sugar, eggs and vanilla with electric mixer.

In a medium mixing bowl, combine flour, baking soda and baking powder. Add flour mixture to creamed mixture. Mix well.

With a wooden spoon, stir in coconut, chocolate chips, raisins or dates, walnuts and oats.

Drop by the spoonful onto a lightly greased baking sheet. Bake at 350° for 12-15 minutes or until lightly browned.

The Lamplighter Bed & Breakfast

602 East Ludington Avenue
Ludington, MI 49431
(800) 301-9792
www.ludington-michigan.com
catsup@aol.com

Hosts: Judy and Heinz Bertram

Combine the European elegance, Victorian tradition and American comfort of The Lamplighter Bed & Breakfast with our attentive AAA 3 Diamond service, and your stay will be unforgettable. Take a stroll along miles of sandy beaches, visit a lighthouse in the park and watch the setting sun dip spectacularly into Lake Michigan. Then relax in a Jacuzzi or dream in front of the fireplace and wake up to the ascending aroma of a gourmet breakfast served in our gazebo or dining room. The only missing ingredient for a romantic escape is YOU.

Rates at the Lamplighter range from $115-$155.
Rates include a full breakfast.

German Sausage Loaf

Based on the overwhelming desire expressed by many of our guests, we have decided to "declassify" our signature recipe for our German Sausage Loaf. This dish is a wonderful addition to any meatless entrée. The addition of "secret" herbs and spices creates an aroma during baking which entices guests to meander to the breakfast table in keen anticipation.

makes 2 loaves, each serving up to 6 guests

---

1 pound roll Jimmy Dean (or equivalent) pork sausage with sage
1 medium apple (Granny Smith or Ida Red)
1 medium red onion
2 cups Pepperidge Farm (or equivalent) stuffing mix
2 large eggs
Herbs de Provence

1 large mixing bowl
2 small loaf pans
1 or 2 serving dishes
grater
aluminum foil
Baking Time: 50-60 minutes
Baking Temperature: 325°

Cut the apple into 4 quarters and remove seeds. Cut ends off onion and peel. Grate both the apple wedges and onion into a large mixing bowl. Pour out excess liquid. Add sausage, eggs and stuffing mix; thoroughly mix by hand until evenly blended.

Spray bottoms of the 2 small loaf pans with nonstick cooking spray and line with a piece of aluminum foil; this will prevent the loaf from sticking to the bottom of the pan and makes removal easier. Spray foil completely with nonstick cooking spray and liberally sprinkle with Herbs de Provence. Tap out excess herbs. Place equal amounts of sausage mix into the two pans and press down to eliminate voids. At this point, depending on the number of servings desired, you can cover one of the pans with aluminum foil and freeze until needed.

Preheat oven to 325°. Place pan(s) in center of preheated oven and bake for 50-60 minutes, until the top is medium brown. Remove pan(s) and pour off any excess grease. Remove sausage loaf by inverting the pan(s). This may require running a knife along the four sides of the pan. Remove and discard the piece of foil from the loaf, cut into 1/2 inch slices, place on a serving dish and garnish with parsley or a rosemary sprig.

When you are ready to use the frozen portion, defrost it overnight in the refrigerator and bake as described above.

Morningside Manor
Bed & Breakfast

3644 North Chippewa (US 31)
Manistee, MI 49660
(888) 419-9668 or (231) 398-9668
www.morningsidebnb.com
pat@morningsidebnb.com

Hosts: Don and Pat Palmbos

This elegant "castle on the hill," located on four acres of trees and rolling hills, is designed to suit your dreams of a perfect relaxing getaway. Each spacious bedroom is tastefully decorated and includes a private bath. A special feature of our home is the beautiful indoor pool and hot tub! The formal living room with fireplace is ideal for a quiet chat or reading a good book from our library. You may also choose the four season knotty pine TV/game room for a friendly get together with the other guests. The "tower suite" is your right choice for a special romantic stay, featuring a private two person whirlpool bath!

We are located near Lake Michigan and the area offers many fine restaurants, golf courses, local beaches, charter fishing, a riverwalk, antique and novelty shops, casino, ski resorts, snowmobiling, and brilliant fall colors.

Rates at Morningside Manor range from $95-$145.
Rates include a full buffet breakfast.

Egg Casserole

This delicious egg casserole is so easy! Make it the night before and bake it in the morning. Because we serve a buffet breakfast, we find it easy to keep on a warmer and still taste wonderful anytime during the hour that we serve. It has been everyone's favorite.

serves 4-6

---

6 eggs
1 can cream of mushroom soup
1/4 cup milk
1 cup shredded cheese
1 cup sausage

Optional Ingredients:
onion
mushrooms
green pepper

1 medium mixing bowl
1- 1 1/2 or 2 quart baking or casserole dish
Baking Time: 50-60 minutes
Baking Temperature: 375°

Using a spoon, blend all ingredients together in medium mixing bowl.

Spray baking or casserole dish with nonstick cooking spray. Pour mixture into prepared dish and cover.

Let set overnight in refrigerator. *Don't* stir before baking. Bake uncovered at 375° for 50-60 minutes.

Royal Rose
Bed & Breakfast

230 Arbutus Avenue
Manistique, MI 49854
(906)341-4886
www.manistique.com
rrbnb@chartermi.net

Hosts: Gilbert and Rosemary Sablack

Enjoy warm hospitality in this 1903 Dutch Colonial home located within walking distance to downtown shopping, marina and the boardwalk along beautiful Lake Michigan. The home features a cozy morning room, two relaxing fireplaces and a large living room. The rooms are elegantly decorated with queen beds, televisions, and private baths. A full candlelight breakfast is served in an extraordinary manner in the formal dining room.

You will feel pampered with the crystal chandeliers, antiques and the charming, distinctive décor. The home is often described as an elegant Bed & Breakfast on an attractive residential street. You will certainly receive the "Royal Treatment" at the Royal Rose Bed & Breakfast.

Rates at the Royal Rose range from $70-$110.
Rates include a full breakfast.

Cappuccino Muffins

Our guests love the flavor combination of chocolate and coffee in these muffins. Not only are they great for breakfast, they make a tasty dessert or evening snack. We receive compliments each time we serve them.

makes 1 dozen muffins

---

2 cups all-purpose flour
3/4 cup sugar
2 1/2 teaspoons baking powder
1 teaspoon ground cinnamon
1/2 teaspoon salt
1 cup milk
2 Tablespoons instant coffee granules
1/2 cup butter or margarine, melted
1 egg, beaten
1 teaspoon vanilla extract
3/4 cup miniature semi-sweet chocolate chips

2 medium mixing bowls
1 muffin pan – 12 count
Baking Time: 17-20 minutes
Baking Temperature: 350°

Preheat oven to 350°. In a bowl, combine flour, sugar, baking powder, cinnamon and salt. In another bowl, stir milk and coffee granules until coffee is dissolved. Add melted butter, egg and vanilla; mix well. Stir into dry ingredients just until moistened. Fold in chocolate chips.

Fill greased or paper-lined muffin cups 2/3 full. Bake at 350° for 17-20 minutes or until muffins test done. Cool for 5 minutes before removing from pan.

The Heather House

409 North Main Street
Marine City, MI 48039
(810)765-3175
www.bluewatertoday.com/heatherhouse/

Hosts: Heather and Bill Bokram

The Heather House, built between 1885 and 1888 for William Sauber, is a very beautiful and elegant Queen Anne style home. William Sauber was chief engineer for the Cleveland Mitchell Fleet of Great Lakes Steamers. He traveled the lakes extensively in the days of the wooden hulled vessels, one of which was named after him. The house remained in the Sauber family for 50 years. After many alterations and years of neglect, the house was purchased and restored to its former beauty by Heather and William Bokram. An addition was added in 1996, and great care was taken to maintain the style and balance of the original structure.

There are four guest rooms, all with private bathrooms and outdoor porches. Some rooms look out on the lovely blue water of the St. Clair River, and others look out on the pretty perennial gardens. The house is very comfortable and filled with antiques and artwork collected by the Bokrams. A full breakfast is a big event, with all homemade goodies guaranteed to keep guests fueled until dinnertime! Canada is a short ferry ride away, and the small Victorian town boasts of several antique stores, small gift shops, an antiquarian bookstore, resale shops and a large Royal Doulton store. Many good restaurants are within five to ten minutes away.

Rates at the Heather House range from $90-$145.
Rates include a full breakfast.

California Strata

This wonderful vegetable strata will become a family favorite! This recipe should be made the night before. We serve the strata with a Mornay sauce and Canadian Pea-meal bacon.

serves 12

---

12 thick slices bread, buttered on one side
2 1/2 cups grated sharp Cheddar cheese
2 cups grated Monterey Jack cheese
3 3/4 cups whole milk
18 eggs, lightly beaten
1 package (10 ounces) chopped frozen spinach, thawed and well drained
1 cup finely sliced sun dried tomatoes
1/2 cup finely shredded fresh basil
1 teaspoon salt
1/2 teaspoon pepper
1 scant teaspoon nutmeg

1 large mixing bowl
1 large baking dish or 1 1/2 cup Pyrex ramekins
Baking Time: 45 minutes total
Baking Temperature: 400°

If using ramekins, cut the bread into 3-inch diameter circles before buttering. Spray dishes with nonstick cooking spray.

Place bread butter side up in dish. Layer spinach, sun dried tomatoes and basil evenly over the bread in the order listed. Top with about 2 Tablespoons of each cheese.

In a large mixing bowl, beat together the eggs, milk and seasonings. Pour over the cheese mix. Cover and place in the refrigerator overnight. Bake in a pre-heated 400° oven for 30 minutes. Cover with foil to prevent the dish from getting too browned. Reduce heat to 350° and continue baking for another 15 minutes.

Serve the strata on warmed serving dishes; if using ramekins, slide the strata out of the dish.

Tip:
The uncooked strata may be frozen for future use. Thaw overnight in the refrigerator before baking the following morning.

The National House Inn

102 South Parkview
Marshall, MI 49068
(269)781-7374
www.nationalhouseinn.com

Host: Barbara Bradley

Built in 1835 as a stagecoach stop, the National House has once again become a haven for weary travelers, and today offers distinctive overnight lodging in a historic setting. Completely and comfortably furnished with antiques from the 19th century, the National House is the oldest operating inn in Michigan.

Rates at the National House Inn range from $105-$145.
Rates include a full breakfast.

National House Strata

This quick and easy recipe is sure to please! The ingredients are easily found in just about any kitchen, so it's the perfect meal for those "drop in" guests.

serves 6

---

3 slices white bread
1/2 teaspoon salt
1/4 teaspoon cream of tartar (optional)
1/2 teaspoon garlic powder
pepper to taste
1 teaspoon oregano
4 eggs
1 3/4 cups half-and-half
3/4 cup shredded Cheddar cheese
1/4 cup grated Romano cheese

1 medium mixing bowl
1 9-inch pie dish
Baking Time: 25 minutes
Baking Temperature: 375°

Preheat oven to 375°. Butter a 9-inch pie dish. Break bread into pieces and spread in dish.

Sprinkle Cheddar cheese over bread. Beat eggs with salt, cream of tartar (optional), and garlic powder. Stir in half-and-half.

Pour mixture over bread. Sprinkle pepper over mixture. Sprinkle oregano over mixture. Sprinkle Romano cheese over mixture.

Bake at 375° for 25 minutes or until puffed and golden brown.

Port City Victorian Inn
Bed & Breakfast

1259 Lakeshore Drive
Muskegon, MI 49441
(231)759-0205
www.portcityinn.com
pcvicinn@gte.net

Hosts: Barb and Fred Schossau

You will feel as if you have stepped through a time portal as you enter through the doors of this 125-year-old historical mansion. This inn features all private baths; some rooms have lake views and two-person double whirlpool baths, queen beds, remote control air conditioning, and one has a beautiful fireplace. The second floor features a rooftop Victorian balcony and a cozy TV room with a view of Muskegon Lake's Lakeshore Yacht Harbor Club.

You will feel at home in the large comfortable dining room and two parlors filled with antiques located on the main floor. The inn is located just five minutes from the white sand beaches of Lake Michigan.

Rates at Port City Victorian Inn range from $100-$150.
Rates include a full breakfast.

Glazed Blueberry Scones

Scones are the inn's favorite sweet treat, a welcome change from muffins. They never seem too heavy, just good eating, and quick to prepare and good tasting with any breakfast that is served. Keeps them coming back for more!

serves 8-12

---

2 cups unbleached flour
1 Tablespoon baking powder
1 teaspoon salt
1/3 cup sugar
1/4 cup butter, cold
3/4 cup buttermilk
1 egg
1 pint fresh blueberries

1 small mixing bowl
1 large mixing bowl
1 double boiler
1 cookie sheet
Baking Time: 15-20 minutes
Baking Temperature: 375°

Preheat oven to 375°. In a large mixing bowl, sift together dry ingredients; mix thoroughly. Cut in butter using pastry blender until mix resembles crumbs. In a small mixing bowl, whisk together buttermilk and egg; add to flour mixture. Mix just to incorporate; do not overwork the dough. Roll blueberries in flour to coat and fold into batter. Drop large Tablespoons of batter onto an ungreased cookie sheet. Bake for 15-20 minutes, until brown. Cool before applying orange glaze.

Orange Glaze

2 Tablespoons butter
2 cups powdered sugar
2 oranges, juiced and zested

Combine butter, sugar, orange zest, and juice in double boiler. Cook until butter and sugar are melted and mixture has thickened. Remove from heat and beat until smooth; cool slightly. Drizzle or brush on top of scones and let glaze get hazy and hardened.

Lisa's Northwoods Bed & Breakfast

12100 East Tatch Road
P.O. Box 229
Omena, MI 49674
(231)271-2010 or (866)269-0683
www.leelanau.com/northwoods
lisamscott@voyager.net

Hosts: Lisa and Tom Scott

Lisa's Northwoods Bed & Breakfast is quietly nestled in the woods just seven miles north of Suttons Bay in the peaceful village of Omena in Leelanau County. Although our home is located in the woods, we are only minutes away from Grand Traverse Bay, Lake Michigan, local eateries and shopping opportunities at the neighboring quaint towns. In the mood for some entertainment or feeling lucky? We are only four miles from the Leelanau Sands Casino. Perhaps sampling wine is your forte? The Leelanau Cellars Winery is only one half mile down the road, not to mention the eleven other wineries in our county.

Our home features three bedrooms, all with private baths, keyed locks, TV/VCR and coffee pots. The Aspen Room has a Jacuzzi tub for two to help create special memories. Full breakfast and evening beverages are served. Please visit our website for more details!

Rates at Lisa's Northwoods range from $70-$125.
Rates include a full breakfast.

Lisa's Strawberry and Amaretto French Toast

Our strawberry and amaretto French toast is a favorite of our customers, especially during the summer months when the strawberries are locally grown and picked. This French toast is like having dessert for breakfast! What a treat! My favorite part is that all the prep work is done the night before so what can be a hectic morning usually turns out to be an easy start to the day. I'm sure this will become a favorite of yours as well...enjoy!

serves 6-8

---

2 loaves Artesian bread, cut into 1 inch thick slices
1 1/2 quarts heavy whipping cream, divided
dash of cinnamon and nutmeg
1/2 cup Leelanau Cellars strawberry wine
2 teaspoons vanilla
9 eggs
1 shot amaretto
2 pints fresh strawberries
1/2 cup sugar

1 small mixing bowl
2 medium mixing bowls
1 large mixing bowl
2 cake pans with covers
2 Air Bake cookie sheets
Baking Time: 20-30 minutes
Baking Temperature: 210°

Cut up bread and let stand several hours to get stale. When bread is ready, combine eggs, 1 quart heavy whipping cream, amaretto, cinnamon, nutmeg and vanilla in a medium mixing bowl. Place bread slices in a shallow cake pan(s) and pour egg/cream mixture over slices. Cover and refrigerate overnight.

Slice and mash strawberries in a large mixing bowl. Stir in wine and sugar. Cover and refrigerate overnight.

Preheat oven to 210°. Gently flip over pieces of bread to coat both sides with egg/cream mixture. Cook pieces on a griddle until golden brown. Transfer bread to Air Bake cookie sheet and bake a minimum of 20 minutes. Sprinkle with powdered sugar and serve with remaining fresh whipped cream and marinated strawberries.

The Canfield House

4138 Portage Point Drive
Onekama, MI 49675
(231)889-5756
www.thecanfieldhouse.com
jane-paul@thecanfieldhouse.com

Hosts: Jane and Paul Mueller

The Canfield House, a lumber baron's 1900 summer retreat, is located on picturesque Portage Lake in the quaint village of Onekama. Leaded glass windows highlight the expansive gathering room with its magnificent stone fireplace and the dining room with Dutch doors that open onto the favorite spot of most guests—a large wraparound porch filled with rockers and porch swings. At the Canfield House, afternoon teas and romantic walks along the beach still happen every day.

Restore the balance to your busy life at this beautiful lakefront Bed & Breakfast. Escape to the natural beauty, privacy and luxury that is the Canfield House.

Rates at the Canfield House range from $95-$145.
Rates include a full breakfast.

Crustless Spinach Quiche

This flavorful quiche is quick and easy! It can be assembled a day in advance or made that morning. It freezes (unbaked) well, too.

serves 8

---

1 pound small curd cottage cheese
1/2 pound Swiss cheese, grated
1/2 pound Kraft Mexican Style Cheddar Jack with jalapeno peppers cheese
4 eggs, beaten
1/2 cup flour
1/2 cup whole milk
1/2 cup (1 stick) butter, melted
1 package (10 ounces) frozen cut leaf spinach, thawed and drained
1 teaspoon baking powder
1/4 teaspoon salt

1 large mixing bowl
1- 9 x 13 inch pan or 7 individual casseroles
Baking Time: 1 hour (for 9x13 pan) or 40 minutes (for individual casseroles)
Baking Temperature: 350°

Preheat oven to 350°. Place all ingredients in a large mixing bowl; mix well. Spread mixture into a greased 9 x 13 inch pan or in 7 individual casseroles. Bake at 350° for 1 hour if using the 9 x 13 pan, or bake for 40 minutes if using individual casseroles.

Cool for 5 minutes before serving.

Another great recipe from The Canfield House......

Apple French Toast

This very simple French toast recipe will get rave reviews! Prepared the night before, your kitchen will be filled with wonderful aromas as your guests and family awaken. Treat yourself anytime with little fuss!

serves 10-12

3/4 cup butter
1 1/2 cups light brown sugar
3 Tablespoons dark corn syrup
4 large apples, peeled, cored and sliced
1 loaf Pepperidge Farm Cinnamon Raisin Bread
8 eggs
2 cups milk
1 1/2 teaspoons vanilla
4 teaspoons tapioca

1 large mixing bowl
1 medium saucepan
1- 9 x 13 inch pan or 7 individual casseroles
Baking Time: 45 minutes
Baking Temperature: 350°

In a medium saucepan, heat the sugar, butter and corn syrup until syrupy. Pour into 7 individual casseroles or a 9 x 13 inch pan. Spread apples over syrup. Cut the crusts off the bread and layer slices of bread over the apples. In a large mixing bowl, beat the remaining ingredients together and pour the mixture over the bread. Refrigerate overnight or freeze for future use.

Bake at 350° for 45 minutes. Drain as necessary.

Another great recipe from The Canfield House......

Broiled Peaches

Some of the most requested recipes here at the Canfield House are for our hot baked fruit dishes. These peaches are super easy and fabulous, with plenty of eye appeal. They're a delicious, tantalizing start to any breakfast.

serves 8-10

---

2 cans (20 ounces) peach halves
1/2 cup brown sugar

Topping:
1/2 cup brown sugar
1/2 cup chopped pecans
1/2 cup (1 stick) melted butter
1/2 cup oatmeal
1/2 cup granola (without dried fruit)
1 cup vanilla yogurt

1 small mixing bowl
1 shallow baking dish

Arrange a single layer of peach halves in a shallow baking dish, rounded sides of peaches facing down. Place 1/2 teaspoon brown sugar in the center of each peach.

Broil for 5 minutes or until all the brown sugar has melted and been absorbed by the peaches. Remove from broiler and place heaping spoonfuls of the topping in the center of each peach.

Place under the broiler again, this time for approximately 3 minutes. Be careful not to burn it! Remove from broiler and top each peach with 1 Tablespoon of vanilla yogurt. Serve warm.

Topping:
Combine all ingredients in a small mixing bowl, excluding yogurt. Mix well. Set aside.

Huron House
Bed & Breakfast

3124 North US 23
Oscoda, MI 48750
(989) 739-9255
www.huronhouse.com
huron@huronhouse.com

Hosts: Denny and Martie Lorenz

Welcome to the Huron House, a luxury retreat for couples. Located on a beautiful sand beach between Tawas and Oscoda, the Huron House features fireplaces, whirlpool tubs, private outdoor hot tubs and breakfast served to your room. Relax and refresh your spirit at the Huron House.

Rates at the Huron House range from $140-180.
Rates include a continental plus breakfast.

Louise's Carrot Bread

This recipe was handed down to me from my mother-in-law. As a young teenager, she was a pastry cook for an exclusive resort. I have served this bread very often at the Huron House, and I'm always asked for the recipe.

serves 36 (3 loaves)

---

3 cups flour
2 cups sugar
1 teaspoon cinnamon
2 teaspoons baking soda
2 cups grated carrots
1 small can pineapple
1 1/2 cups vegetable oil
3 eggs, slightly beaten
2 teaspoons vanilla
2 Tablespoons grated orange rind
1 1/2 cups chopped walnuts
1 cup coconut

1 large mixing bowl
1 wooden spoon
3 medium loaf pans
Baking Time: 45 minutes
Baking Temperature: 350°

Mix all dry ingredients in a large mixing bowl. Add carrots, pineapple (juice and fruit), oil, eggs and vanilla, mixing well after each ingredient. Add orange rind, nuts and coconut. Mix well. Pour in greased and floured loaf pans; fill pans 1/2 to 3/4 full.

Bake at 350° for 45 minutes or until top is set.

The Candlewyck House
Bed & Breakfast

438 East Lowell
P.O. Box 392
Pentwater, MI 49449
(231) 869-5967
www.candlewyckhouse.com

Hosts: John and Mary Jo Neidow

    The Candlewyck House is an unusual blend of colonial and contemporary American style. Our six romantic rooms offer more than enough amenities to spoil even the most experienced traveler. Guests especially enjoy our fireplace suites with mini kitchens and a flower filled patio, perfect for sipping early morning coffee or afternoon wine. A library of more than 1,000 volumes awaits those dedicated bibliophiles, and for action packed moments, there are over 300 videos to choose from. We invite you to join our table, and while partaking of our full country breakfast, enjoy stimulating conversation with your fellow travelers.

    After more than 13 years of being innkeepers, we still look forward to each new season. Because we are only a short walk to our pristine Lake Michigan beach and a quaint boutique-filled downtown, our guests often park their cars and join us for a step back in time while visiting Historic Pentwater.

Rates at the Candlewyck House range from $99-$129.
Rates include a full country breakfast.

Raspberry Bread

This bread is best if made a day ahead so it can mature. It can also be frozen for up to 2 months.

makes 1 loaf

---

1 package (10 ounces) frozen raspberries in light syrup, thawed
2 eggs
1/2 cup & 2 Tablespoons safflower oil
1 cup sugar
1 1/2 cups white flour
1 teaspoon cinnamon
1 teaspoon baking soda

1 medium mixing bowl
electric mixer
1 9x5 inch loaf pan
Baking Time: 55-60 minutes
Baking Temperature: 350°

Preheat oven to 350°. Puree raspberries with their syrup; strain and discard seeds. Place eggs, oil and sugar in bowl. Mix with an electric mixer for 3 minutes at medium speed. Add raspberry puree and blend well. Add flour, cinnamon and baking soda and mix for 1 minute on low speed.

Bake in greased 9x5 inch loaf pan for 55-60 minutes. Cool 30 minutes. Remove from pan and cool completely. Wrap tightly in plastic wrap.

Pentwater Abbey
Bed & Breakfast

85 West First Street
P.O. Box 735
Pentwater, MI 49449
(231)869-4094
www.bbonline.com/mi/abbey/
waytogomk@qcinet.net

Hosts: Marv and Karen Way

Pentwater is a delightful village reminiscent of earlier times. Guests enjoy the quiet and relaxing atmosphere.

Built in 1868, the Abbey reflects the Victorian ambience with its handcarved cherrywood fireplaces. It is located 1 block from downtown, across the street from Pentwater Lake and just 3 blocks from the beautiful Lake Michigan beach.

Many guests walk to the beach, downtown shops and restaurants. Others enjoy the use of our bicycles. For the comfort and enjoyment of our guests, all three rooms have private bathrooms, cable TV and air conditioning. Upon arriving, guests are greeted with coffee and homemade cookies. A full breakfast is served.

Rates at the Pentwater Abbey range from $75-$110.
Rates include a full breakfast.

Glazed Bacon with Walnuts

This bacon is so yummy; you will love it! It is very, very easy and quick to make. Our returning guests that have had it always request that I make it again. I serve it with eggs and muffins.

serves 6-8

---

1 pound bacon, sliced
1/4 cup packed dark brown sugar
1 teaspoon flour
1/2 cup walnuts, chopped

1 small mixing bowl
1 large oven broiler pan
1 large platter
Baking Time: 30 minutes
Baking Temperature: 350°

Preheat oven to 350°. Spray broiler pan with nonstick cooking spray. Arrange bacon slices closely together, but not overlapping, on broiler pan. In a small mixing bowl, mix chopped walnuts, brown sugar and flour. Mix well. Sprinkle the walnut mixture evenly over the bacon.

Bake until crisp and brown, about 30 minutes. Start checking the bacon after 15 minutes to be sure that it doesn't burn.

Drain the bacon on paper toweling. Serve with eggs, muffins and/or toast. This recipe is great reheated.

Serenity
A Bed & Breakfast

504 Rush Street
Petoskey, MI 49770
(877)347-6171 or (231)347-6171
www.serenitybb.com
stay@serenitybb.com

Hosts: David and Peggy Vermeesch

Serenity, our beautiful turn-of-the-century home, is located high on a hill overlooking Little Traverse Bay. Serenity was designed and built by the first architect in Petoskey 100 years ago. There are lovely oak hardwood floors and charming touches to make your stay with us a memorable one.

This charming 1890s Victorian Bed & Breakfast is four blocks from downtown Petoskey. Antiques, soft music and lace complete the ambience of casual elegance. Each of the three rooms has a queen bed, private bath and air conditioning. Exceptional hospitality will make your stay unforgettable. Serenity has been featured in *Time* Magazine, *Michigan Living,* and Mary Engelbreit's *Home Companion* Magazine. We're open all year.

Rates at Serenity range from $115-$145.
Rates include a full breakfast.

Zesty Sausage Mini Quiches

This tasty mini quiche is quick and easy to prepare with few ingredients. "Real men" do eat and love this quiche. It is great served with your favorite potato dish.

serves 6

---

1 package (16 ounces) spicy breakfast sausage, such as Bob Evans Zesty or
     Jimmy Dean Hot
3 eggs
8 ounces cream cheese
1 package (6 ounces) "flaky" biscuits (Grands or Large)
4 ounces shredded Cheddar cheese

1 small mixing bowl
1 medium frying pan
1 6-servings size Texas (Large) muffin pan
6 regular 8-inch breakfast plates

Brown the sausage the night before assembling the quiches. Drain well and crumble into small pieces. Refrigerate.

In the morning, mix softened cream cheese and eggs (add one at a time). Blend well after each egg is added.

Separate each large biscuit into three layers and press into bottom of each lightly greased muffin tin.

Sprinkle about 1/4 cup sausage over biscuit. Spoon 2-3 Tablespoons cream cheese mixture over sausage. Sprinkle enough Cheddar cheese over the quiches to cover the tops completely.

Bake according to biscuit package instructions plus 2 minutes.

Sprinkle the top with paprika, minced fresh parsley or snipped dill.

932 Penniman
A Bed & Breakfast

932 Penniman Avenue
Plymouth, MI 48170
(734)414-7444
www.bbonline.com/mi/penniman

Hosts: Carey and Jon Gary

932 Penniman stands at the gateway to fashionable tree lined Penniman Avenue in a neighborhood of elegant classic homes. One short block away, the city of Plymouth offers fine specialty shops, restaurants, galleries, picturesque Kellogg Park and even a neighborhood movie theater which still serves real butter on the popcorn! Plymouth is also home to numerous festivals and gatherings such as the International Ice Spectacular and Art in the Park. Enjoy the small town charm and hospitality which is Plymouth.

Spend a night or a weekend in this 1903 historical home which combines the elements of Queen Anne Victorian, Arts and Crafts and Neo-Gothic architectural styles. Enjoy the sweeping oak staircase, hidden pocket doors, seven bay windows and original oak woodwork.

Watch your favorite program or a movie on the large screen TV in the parlor or cozy up by the fireplace in the reception hall. Enjoy a book or the stereo in the library. Each area is a comfortable spot for reading, playing games, listening to music or catnapping.

Rates at 932 Penniman range from $125-$225.
Rates include a full breakfast.

English Scramble

This is a very flavorful, hearty breakfast entrée. Even though it is served on an English muffin, it is loaded with protein for those low carb diets. I use my own sausage recipe, but any zesty sausage or ham will do. Without meat, it will even make some vegetarians happy. Makes a great Sunday buffet dish.

serves 2

---

8 ounces bulk breakfast sausage
4 mushrooms, sliced
1/4 cup red peppers, diced
1/4 cup green peppers, diced
1 green onion, minced
1 Roma tomato, peeled, seeded, diced
4 ounces butter, divided
4 eggs
2 English muffins, toasted
8 ounces Colby/Monterey Jack cheese, shredded
salsa to accompany

1 small mixing bowl
2-8 inch sauté pans
broiler
2 dinner plates

Brown sausage; drain grease. Wash and prepare vegetables. Sauté in one half of the butter. Add cooked sausage. In a small mixing bowl, scramble eggs. Add to meat/vegetable mixture and cook until just set.

Toast and butter English muffins.

Spoon one fourth of the egg mixture over each muffin half. Top with one fourth of the cheese and melt under broiler.

Serve with your favorite salsa.

Stafford House
Bed & Breakfast

4489 Main
P.O. Box 204
Port Hope, MI 48468
(989)428-4554
www.staffordhousepthope.com
staffordhouse@centurytel.net

Hosts: Greg and Kathy Gephart

Enjoy comfort and peace at the Stafford House in the quaint village of Port Hope—"the little town with the big welcome." The Stafford House was built by lumber baron W.R. Stafford as a wedding present to his daughter in 1886. He spared no expense, with beautiful woodworking and two fireplaces of Italianate marble. We have four guest rooms with private baths. We are located less than 1/2 mile from beautiful Lake Huron. Nearby Pointe Aux Barques Lighthouse is one of the few working lighthouses in Michigan.

Rates at the Stafford House range from $65-$90.
Rates include a full buffet style breakfast.

Easy Egg Brunch

"That was good!" exclaimed our guest who was hoping her husband would enjoy their stay at a Bed & Breakfast, especially when it would be his first time and did not know what to expect when it came to breakfast. After giving out the recipe, our guest called and told us that she didn't know an easy recipe could have so much taste.

serves 8-10

---

1 package (24 ounces) hash brown potato patties
1/4 cup melted butter
1 pound ground sausage
1 cup Cheddar cheese, shredded
1 cup mozzarella cheese, shredded
8 eggs
1 cup milk
1/4 teaspoon seasoned salt

1 small dish
1 medium mixing bowl
1 skillet
1- 9 x 13 inch pan
Baking Time: 30-40 minutes
Baking Temperature: 350°

Place hash browns in 9 x 13 inch pan. Pour butter over hash browns and bake at 425° for 20 minutes. Brown and drain sausage. Spread over potatoes and sprinkle cheeses on top. Beat eggs, milk and seasoned salt together. Spread over cheese.

Bake in a 350° oven for 30-40 minutes until set and golden brown.

Another great recipe from the Stafford House...

Miniature Sausage Muffins

Using a mini muffin pan has never been so fun! This unique recipe is fun to make and fun to eat. Be sure to serve it with honey butter for a different twist.

makes 2 1/2 dozen mini muffins

1/2 pound bulk pork sausage
1/3 cup chopped green onions
1 1/2 cups package biscuit mix
1/2 teaspoon dry mustard
1/4 teaspoon pepper
1/2 cup milk
1/2 cup (2 ounces) finely shredded Cheddar cheese

Honey Butter:
1/4 cup & 2 Tablespoons butter, softened
2/3 cup honey
1/2 teaspoon grated lemon peel

1 medium mixing bowl
1 skillet
2 mini muffin pans
Baking Time: 12-14 minutes
Baking Temperature: 400°

Preheat oven to 400°. Combine sausage and green onions in a skillet; cook over medium heat until sausage is browned, stirring to crumble. Drain well.

In a medium mixing bowl, combine biscuit mix, dry mustard and pepper; add milk, stirring until moist. Stir in sausage mixture and cheese (mixture will be thick).

Spoon mixture into greased mini muffin pans, filling 2/3 full. Bake at 400° for 12-14 minutes or until golden brown. Serve warm with honey butter, if desired.

Honey Butter:
Mix butter, honey and lemon peel together. Chill for several hours.

Another great recipe from the Stafford House...

Scalloped Apple

This is good alone or as a topping for French toast, pancakes or oatmeal. The recipe can be doubled or tripled as needed.

serves 2

---

1 large baking apple, peeled and thinly sliced
2 Tablespoons melted butter
1 teaspoon flour
1 1/2 Tablespoons dark brown sugar
1/4 teaspoon ground cinnamon
1 Tablespoon lemon juice

1 small mixing bowl
1 1-quart baking dish
Baking Time: 20-25 minutes
Baking Temperature: 350°

Preheat oven to 350°.

Arrange apple slices along bottom of baking dish, overlapping the slices.

In a small mixing bowl, combine remaining ingredients.

Brush butter mixture over apple slices.

Bake at 350° for 20-25 minutes. Serve warm.

Davidson House
Bed & Breakfast

1707 Military Street
Port Huron, MI 48060
(810)987-3922
www.davidsonhouse.com

Hosts: Mark and Odette LaPrairie

This grand Queen Anne Victorian (circa 1888) sits in the tranquil Military Street Home District, across the street from the St. Clair River and Canada. Steeped in history (the first home electrified in Port Huron) and listed on the National Historic Register, this stately home features high ceilings, fancy plasterwork, rich woodwork, stain-jeweled and leaded glass windows, seven fireplaces and antiques. The parlor and sitting room are finished in butternut. A large open oak staircase is showcased in the foyer. Four private guest bedrooms all have private baths, quilted four-poster beds, claw foot tubs and bubble bath. One boasts a double Jacuzzi and balcony overlooking flower gardens and the river.

A delicious full breakfast is served with a Victorian setting, vintage lace and linens, and is accented by flowers and candles. The oldest lighthouse in Michigan, Fort Gratiot Lighthouse, is only 2 miles away, and beautiful downtown Port Huron is a mere 10 blocks from our doorstep.

Rates at the Davidson House range from $100-$150.
Rates include a full breakfast.

Pumpkin Swirl Cake

This is a delicious cake with a great presentation. It only takes 15 minutes to bake! It was the winning dessert recipe in our holiday cookbook for the Port Huron newspaper.

serves 8-10

3/4 cup all purpose flour
1 teaspoon baking powder
1 teaspoon cinnamon
1/4 teaspoon salt
3 large eggs
1 cup sugar
2/3 cup canned pumpkin

Filling:
8 ounces cream cheese—set aside 2 Tablespoons for frosting
1/3 cup sugar
1 large egg
1 Tablespoon milk

Frosting:
2 Tablespoons cream cheese
2 Tablespoons margarine
powdered sugar (used to adjust consistency)

3 medium mixing bowls
1 large mixing bowl
1 15x10x1 inch jelly roll pan
wax paper
8-10 dessert plates
Baking Time: 15 minutes
Baking Temperature: 375°.

Preheat oven to 375°. Grease, or lightly spray with nonstick cooking spray, the jelly roll pan. Line pan with wax paper, then lightly grease or spray the wax paper. Prepare the filling as described below, place in prepared pan and refrigerate while mixing the rest of the recipe.

In a medium mixing bowl, sift together flour, baking powder, cinnamon and salt. Set aside. In a large mixing bowl, beat the eggs for 3 minutes on high. Add sugar and slowly beat 3 more minutes. Sugar will almost be dissolved. Stir in pumpkin and mix well. Fold the pumpkin mixture into the flour mixture. Spread evenly over the cream cheese mixture in the pan.

Bake for 15 minutes or until the top of the cake springs back. Immediately loosen the sides of the cake from the pan and invert cake on linen towel sprinkled with powdered sugar. Peel off wax paper. Roll up the cake from the short side (like a jelly roll) using the towel to help roll the cake. Cool on a wire rack and frost when the cake is cooled.

Filling:
In a medium mixing bowl, beat the cream cheese and sugar on high until smooth. Beat in egg and milk. Spread evenly in bottom of jelly roll pan that is lined with greased wax paper as described above and refrigerate.

Frosting:
In a medium mixing bowl, beat cream cheese and margarine until well blended. Add powdered sugar to adjust consistency, if desired.

William Hopkins Manor
Bed & Breakfast

613 North Riverside Avenue
Saint Clair, MI 48079
(810)329-0188
whmanor@aol.com

Hosts: Sharon Llewellyn and Terry Mazzarese

William Hopkins Manor is a Bed & Breakfast in an elegant 1876 Second Empire Victorian home. Perched on a hill across from the St. Clair River, the manor transports guests back in time.

Guests can enjoy a casual five-minute walk into St. Clair to dine at the historic St. Clair Inn or delight in fares offered by other fine St. Clair restaurants. Back at the manor, guests enjoy pleasant conversation in several of the elegant rooms available. A crackling fire that warms a cold winter evening invites you to sip a mug of hot cocoa. On the front porch, enjoy a quiet summer night watching international freighters navigate the St. Clair River.

Step into history at Williams Hopkins Manor. Enjoy some time away reliving times when life was leisurely. Relax and unwind as our guest. Go golfing or antiquing, go for a boat ride or a picnic. Catch up on your reading or play some billiards. Take a nice long, lazy nap or pamper yourself with a massage. After all, this is your special time.

We are proud to offer a healthy, smoke-free environment.

Rates at Williams Hopkins Manor range from $80-$100.
Rates include a full breakfast.

Apple Harvest Salad

This fruit dish is a "refreshing" change. We especially enjoy serving it in the fall to celebrate the fresh Michigan apple harvest. We like to use four different apples. Using one yellow, one green and two red apples gives nice color to the salad. This fruit salad complements almost any main entrée. We often serve it with stuffed French toast. It takes about 10 minutes to prepare.

serves 8-10

1 cup plain yogurt
2 Tablespoons sugar
2 Tablespoons Miracle Whip
1/2 teaspoon vanilla
1/2 teaspoon cinnamon (or to taste)
5 Tablespoons chopped walnuts
handful of raisins
4 large apples (use different varieties)
1 can (20 ounces) pineapple chunks

1 medium mixing bowl

Mix first 7 ingredients in a medium mixing bowl. Slice, core and cut apples into chunks. Add to mixture.

Drain pineapple and reserve juice for your own treat. Add drained pineapple to mixture and toss gently.

Keep salad chilled until ready to use.

South Cliff Inn
Bed & Breakfast

1900 Lakeshore Drive
Saint Joseph, MI 49085
(269)983-4881
www.southcliffinn.com

Host: Bill Swisher

South Cliff Inn Bed & Breakfast is an English cottage style Bed & Breakfast. The exterior of the inn is English cottage style with decks overlooking Lake Michigan, a beautiful formal garden and sunsets beyond compare. The interior of the inn is English country style with many antiques, imported fabrics and custom designed furnishings. Some of the guest rooms have fireplaces and/or whirlpool tubs, and several even have balconies that overlook Lake Michigan. The seven guest rooms are individually decorated, each with a private bath. The atmosphere of the inn is one of warmth and friendliness. The homemade breakfasts are created by the retired chef and owner and are something that you will not want to miss.

South Cliff Inn Bed & Breakfast has received, for the seventh year, *The Readers' Choice Award for Favorite Bed & Breakfast in Southwestern Michigan.* South Cliff Inn has been distinguished from other Bed & Breakfasts by being cited as *one of 40 ways to pamper yourself* in *Chicago Magazine* and listed under *Good nights lodgings you'll like along the way* in *Midwest Living Magazine*.

The inn is located 1 mile south of the quaint downtown area of Saint Joseph which has wonderful shops, restaurants and entertainment. The beaches in this area are some of the most beautiful you will ever come upon. Wineries, nature centers, museums, restaurants and antique shopping are all a very short and scenic drive from South Cliff Inn. We strive to make your stay at South Cliff Inn Bed & Breakfast a most enjoyable and relaxing experience.

Rates at the South Cliff Inn range from $85-$215.
Rates include a continental plus breakfast.

Blackberry Crisp

I found this recipe in a very old cookbook from a local church. I like old time "comfort food," and this recipe definitely fits that category. Guests always rave about this recipe. I have used either peaches or blueberries in this recipe instead of the blackberries, and all are delicious. And it's easy and fast to make.

serves 8-10

4-5 cups blackberries, fresh or frozen
2 Tablespoons flour
3/4 cup sugar
1/4 pound butter, melted

Topping:
1 cup flour
1 cup sugar
1 teaspoon baking powder
1 egg, beaten

1 9 1/2 inch deep mixing bowl
1 smaller bowl for topping
1- 8 1/2 x 11-inch glass casserole dish or smaller deep dish casserole
Baking Time: 45-60 minutes
Baking Temperature: 350°

Preheat oven to 350° . Gently toss fruit with flour and sugar and put in baking dish that has been sprayed with nonstick cooking spray. Sprinkle topping over fruit evenly. Drizzle melted butter over the topping.

Bake uncovered until top is browned and fruit is bubbling.

Topping:
Combine all ingredients with a spoon until crumbly.

Sherwood Forest
Bed & Breakfast

938 Center Street   P.O. Box 893
Saugatuck, MI 49453   Douglas, MI 49406
(800)838-1246 or (269)857-1246
www.sherwoodforestbandb.com

Hosts: Keith and Sue Charak

This Saugatuck Bed and Breakfast offers luxury. Hardwood floors, leaded-glass windows and wraparound porch add to ideal surroundings. Guest rooms offer antiques, cozy wing chairs, private baths, queen-size beds, and air conditioning. Sherwood Forest has two suites available with Jacuzzi and fireplace. One room sports a hand-painted mural that transforms the room into a canopied tree loft and is complemented by a gas fireplace. Outside is a heated pool adorned with a hand-painted mural of a sunken Greek ship embedded in a coral reef. Walk one half block to a Lake Michigan beach and beautiful sunsets. In winter, cross-country ski or hike along wooded paths.

Experience the true Michigan Bed and Breakfast experience at Sherwood Forest.

Rates at Sherwood Forest are $85.
Rates include a full breakfast.

Ringo's Corn Muffins

This is one of the best combinations for corn muffins Ms. Sue has created, and we've named it after one of our best buddies, Ringo, one of the grooviest kids on the planet. They have joined the ranks of the muffin brigade that we serve here in The Forest. Yum, yum, eat'em up!

serves 12

2 eggs
1/2 cup low fat cottage cheese
1/2 cup light sour cream
2 Tablespoons butter, melted
3/4 teaspoon salt
1/4 cup finely chopped onion
1 cup frozen corn, cooked
1 package (8 1/2 ounces) corn muffin mix

1 small mixing bowl
1 large mixing bowl
1 muffin baking tin for 12 muffins
1 wooden spoon
Baking Time: 15-20 minutes
Baking Temperature: 400°

Preheat oven to 400°. In a large mixing bowl, combine muffin mix, corn, onion and salt. In a small mixing bowl, beat eggs. Add cottage cheese, sour cream and butter to egg mixture. Fold liquid mixture into dry ingredients; stir until moistened. Do not overmix.

Fill greased or lined muffins cups 2/3 full. Bake for 15-20 minutes.

Twin Gables Inn

900 Lake Street
P.O. Box 1150
Saugatuck, MI 49453
(269)857-4346 or (800)231-2185
www.twingablesinn.com
relax@twingablesinn.com

Hosts: Bob Lawrence and Susan Schwaderer

This state registered historic Bed & Breakfast began as the Twin Gables Hotel & Restaurant during the prohibition era. Local legend claims that Al Capone stayed here while using Saugatuck as a port for transporting spirits into Chicago. Our casually elegant inn is perfect for that romantic getaway. Relax on the four-season porch while enjoying calming water views and spectacular sunsets over Lake Kalamazoo. Several of the 14 guestrooms include gas fireplaces—all with private bathrooms and furnished with antiques and reproductions. A served, gourmet breakfast welcomes you each morning with homemade treats at night. Enjoy the common area's wood burning fireplace or unwind in the large indoor hot tub. Stroll the gardens and pond on our two rolling acres or swim in the outdoor pool in the summer. Enjoy the short walk to shops and galleries.

Rates at Twin Gables Inn range from $75-$185.
Rates include a full gourmet breakfast.

Southwestern Hash Brown Quiche
(a.k.a. Cowboy Quiche—the quiche that real men eat!)

Our guests—and Sue's mom—love this quiche! Using turkey sausage and 2% milk, it is lighter than many breakfast entrées, too. Your vegetarian friends will enjoy it equally well when you omit the sausage. It is easy to make and can be made ahead of time. It also reheats well. Serve with cornbread or muffins.

serves 6

---

3 cups frozen shredded hash brown potatoes
1/4 pound sausage (we use Mexican-flavored ground turkey)
4 Tablespoons chilies, diced
1/3 cup red bell pepper, diced
1/3 cup Roma tomatoes, diced
1/2 cup green onions, sliced, divided—use 1/4 cup for garnish
1 1/2 cups Mozzarella cheese, shredded
1/2 teaspoon white pepper
1 cup 2% milk
4 large eggs, slightly beaten
1/2 cup salsa—for garnish
1 orange, cut into 6 slices—for garnish

1 medium frying pan
1 quiche or pie pan
1 small mixing bowl
Baking Time: 50-60 minutes
Baking Temperature: 350°

Preheat oven to 425°. Spray pie pan with nonstick cooking spray. Add hash browns, spreading across the bottom and sides of the pan. Bake for 25-30 minutes or until lightly browned on edges. Cool.

Brown sausage. Drain and crumble.

Dice vegetables (chilies, bell pepper, tomatoes). Slice onions. Spread vegetables—using only 1/4 cup onions—over potato crust in pie pan. Add sausage, then cheese. Sprinkle with pepper.

Cover with plastic wrap and refrigerate until baking time (recipe thus far can be made the day before).

Preheat oven to 350 °. Remove plastic wrap from pan. In a small mixing bowl, mix eggs and milk together with whisk. Pour over ingredients in pan. Bake for 50-60 minutes or until lightly browned and knife inserted in the center comes out clean.

Let stand for 10 minutes. Cut into 6 servings. Using pie server, place each serving in the center of a plate. Place an orange slice on one side and a dollop of salsa on the other side. Sprinkle green onions on the top of the quiche and on top of the orange slice.

Twin Oaks Inn

227 Griffith Street
P.O. Box 818
Saugatuck, MI 49453
(269)857-1600
www.bbonline.com/mi/twinoaks
twinoaks@sirus.com

Host: Willa Lemken

What was a 19th century lumberman's boarding house is now an elegant and charming Bed & Breakfast. The inn is nestled at the foot of Hoffman Street Hill on a quiet street in downtown Saugatuck with easy access to shopping, restaurants, art galleries, antiques and all area activities.

Rates at Twin Oaks Inn range from $95-$135.
Rates include a full breakfast.

Twin Oaks Inn Asparagus Quiche

This unique, light and fluffy quiche just melts in your mouth!

serves 6-8

8-10 asparagus stalks, blanched, cut into 1 inch pieces
1/4 cup Feta cheese
6 eggs
3 Tablespoons flour
2 cups milk
1 ready made pie crust
1/8 teaspoon nutmeg

1 medium mixing bowl
1- 8 or 9 inch pie plate
Baking Time: 45-50 minutes
Baking Temperature: 350°

Preheat oven to 350°. In a medium mixing bowl, beat 3 eggs and flour. Beat in remaining eggs, then beat in milk. Set aside.

Arrange asparagus in prepared pie crust. Sprinkle with Feta cheese. Pour egg mixture over asparagus and cheese.

Bake 45-50 minutes or until silver knife inserted in center of quiche comes out clean.

Let quiche set for 10 minutes before serving.

Inn at Black Star Farms

10844 East Revold Road
Suttons Bay, MI 49682
(231)271-4970 ext. 150
www.blackstarfarms.com
innkeeper@blackstarfarms.com

Host: Caryn Anderson

Our inn is nestled below a hillside of vineyards on a working farm with a producing winery/distillery and creamery. Its seven contemporary guest rooms, some with fireplaces and Jacuzzis, each with private bath, have fine furniture, luxurious linens, down comforters and plenty of pillows. Amenities include our house wine, cozy robes and in-room satellite television. Sauna and massage services are available, as well as a seasonal indoor pool.

We are in the heart of the Leelanau Wine Trail, and nearby attractions include Sleeping Bear Dunes National Lakeshore, Interlochen Center for the Arts, quaint villages, shops and galleries. There are numerous recreational possibilities in every season including hiking, cycling, snowshoeing and cross-country skiing on our own trails. Our stables are able to board your horse during your stay.

Rates at the Inn at Black Star Farms range from $100-$270.
Rates include a full gourmet breakfast.

Eggs Havana Style

Eggs Havana Style adds a new twist to breakfast, leaving the old standard eggs behind for a day. This great recipe adds a little spice and exciting flavors to an egg dish with easy preparation. Serve this entrée right in the ramekin on a plate with your favorite potatoes and breakfast meat.

serves 4

1/4 cup olive oil
1 small onion, finely chopped
1 small green bell pepper, finely chopped
2 cloves garlic, finely chopped
1 cup tomatoes, drained and finely chopped
1/2 cup pimiento, drained and finely chopped
2 Tablespoons dry sherry
salt and pepper to taste
8 large eggs
4 Tablespoons butter
chopped parsley for garnish

1 medium skillet
1 saucer
4 ramekins or au gratin dishes
Baking Time: 10-12 minutes
Baking Temperature: 350 °

In a medium skillet over low heat, heat oil until it is fragrant; add onion, bell pepper and garlic. Cook until tender, about 8-10 minutes.

Add tomatoes, pimientos and sherry; cook until thickened, about 15 minutes.

Season with salt and pepper.

Lightly oil ramekins or au gratin dishes and divide the mixture among them.

For each dish, break 2 eggs into a saucer then slide them on top of mixture in dishes. Drizzle with 1 Tablespoon butter.

Bake until whites are set and yolks are soft, about 10-12 minutes. Sprinkle with salt, pepper and parsley. Before serving, place on a serving plate to protect the table.

Korner Kottage
Bed & Breakfast

503 North St. Josephs Avenue
P.O. Box 174
Suttons Bay, MI 49682
(231)271-2711
www.kornerkottage.com
info@kornerkottage.com

Host: Sharon Sutterfield

The lake stone screened porch of this restored 1920s Craftsman style home reflects an idyllic, quaint charm. Upon arrival, guests feel the warmth of this home, just as your innkeeper felt when purchasing the home four years ago. Located in a Nordic village on the Leelanau Peninsula, only a few steps will take you back in time to explore unique shops, theater, restaurants and the crystal clear, blue bay.

Relax in an inviting living room, appointed with warmth and comfort. In the warm months, the front screened porch is a popular gathering place; catching a glimpse of busy hummingbirds in the perennial garden is also a favorite.

Cheery guest bedrooms are known for their comfortable beds, ironed linens and uncluttered, crisp, clean appearance. Your innkeeper enjoys the preparation and presentation of a hearty, appealing breakfast, served with a smile in the dining room each morning. Memorable surroundings and warm hospitality awaits each and every guest!

Rates at Korner Kottage range from $90-$140.
Rates include a full breakfast.

Gram's French Apple Pie

This wonderful pie was passed down from my grandmother who farmed apple and cherry orchards with my grandfather in northern Michigan. One of my high school friends from the '70s brought her youngest son to my mom's for a visit several years ago. He gobbled down a piece ala mode and politely declined a second piece but picked up his plate and licked it clean! My friends live in North Carolina now, so when I visit, I pack my recipe, bake them a pie, and we all laugh about who will be the first to lick their plate!

serves 6-8

---

1 unbaked pie shell
1 cup sugar, divided
1/2 cup plus 1 Tablespoon flour, divided
4 Green Delicious apples, peeled and sliced
4 Granny Smith apples, peeled and sliced (you can use any firm baking apples)
2 teaspoons lemon juice
2/3 cup sugar
pinch of salt
1/2 teaspoon cinnamon
1/4 teaspoon nutmeg
2/3 stick unsalted butter

1 small mixing bowl
1 large mixing bowl
1 8 or 9 inch pie pan
Baking Time: 40-50 minutes
Baking Temperature: 400°

Preheat oven to 400°. Line pie pan with unbaked pie crust. Sprinkle 1/3 cup sugar and 1 Tablespoon flour on the bottom of the crust.

Place peeled and sliced apples in a large bowl, sprinkle them with lemon juice, toss and place in pie crust.

In a small mixing bowl, add 2/3 cup sugar, 1/2 cup flour, pinch of salt, cinnamon, nutmeg and softened butter. Work together until crumbly. Carefully add this mixture on top of the apples, covering the entire top.

Bake in a 400° oven for 40-50 minutes or until the top is brown.

Aberdeen Stone Cottage
Bed & Breakfast

315 North Elmwood
Traverse City, MI 49684
(231)935-3715
www.aberdeenstonecottage.com
aberdeen@chartermi.net

Hosts: Bill and Bonnie Mathias

Enjoy the Grand Traverse region from our charming and convenient location. Find yourself steps away from bayfront parks and beaches, within easy access to a bike trail system and minutes from downtown shopping and dining. Use Aberdeen Stone Cottage as a base to explore everything the city and environs have to offer—the celebratory bustle of the Cherry Festival, quiet days at the beach, or visits to area golf courses or ski slopes.

Rates at Aberdeen Stone Cottage range from $75-$95.
Rates include a full breakfast.

Scottish Oatmeal Scones

This is our favorite scone recipe because it is delicious, quick and easy to make. We use a baking stone, but a cookie sheet could function as well. Any dried, fresh or frozen fruits can be substituted, and sometimes we also add nuts. It is nice to serve the scones with homemade cherry preserves on the side. We are pleased that our guests frequently ask for a copy of this recipe.

makes 10 scones

---

1 1/2 cups flour
1 1/4 cups old-fashioned oatmeal, uncooked
1/4 cup sugar
1 Tablespoon baking powder
1 teaspoon cream of tartar
1/4 teaspoon salt
2/3 cup butter, melted
1/3 cup milk
1 egg, beaten
1/2 cup dried cherries

1 medium mixing bowl
1 large mixing bowl
1 baking stone or cookie sheet
Baking Time: 12 minutes
Baking Temperature: 425°

Preheat oven to 425°. In a large mixing bowl, combine dry ingredients and mix lightly with a fork.

In a medium mixing bowl, mix milk and eggs together. Pour mixture into dry ingredients. Add melted butter and cherries, stirring just until ingredients are moistened.

Turn out onto a baking stone or cookie sheet prepared with about 1/4 cup flour. Work flour in by lightly kneading until dry enough to just handle. Flatten into an approximately seven inch circle. Dough will be wet.

Cut into 10 wedge-shaped pieces, moving scones about one inch apart. Re-shape wedges, pat with melted butter and sprinkle with sugar.

Bake at 425° for 12 minutes or until lightly browned.

Field of Dreams
Bed & Breakfast

15627 Center Road
Traverse City, MI 49686
(231)223-7686
www.pentel.net/fieldofdreams
field@pentel.net

Hosts: Dennis and Sue Field

Field of Dreams Bed & Breakfast is located on one of the most beautiful peninsulas in Michigan. Filled with orchards and vineyards, it is sometimes referred to as "little Napa Valley." Our home is spacious and comfortable with a warm country décor. Our third story viewing tower is a must to visit while here. The three-course breakfasts are completely homemade and our guests love them. I love them because they are unique and fairly easy to prepare.

Rates at Field of Dreams range from $100-$125.
Rates include a full breakfast.

Fruit and Cherry Parfait

This fruit and yogurt dish is our most popular. Many of our returning guests request it ahead of time. It's easy to prepare and even non-yogurt lovers like it if they're daring enough to try!

serves 6

---

2 containers (8 ounces each) vanilla yogurt (such as Dannon Light)
Fresh fruit—blueberries, raspberries or chopped strawberries
star fruit or kiwi, cut into 6 slices
granola (see recipe below)
mint sprigs

Cherry Granola:
1 1/4 cup old fashioned oats
1/2 cup chopped walnuts
1/4 cup flaked coconut
1/4 cup pure maple syrup (or Mrs. Butterworth's)
1 teaspoon ground cinnamon
1 teaspoon vanilla
1/3 cup dried cherries
1 Tablespoon corn syrup

6 champagne glasses
1- 9 x 13 x 2-inch baking pan
1 saucepan
Baking Time: 30 minutes(granola)
Baking Temperature: 275° (granola)

Using 6 champagne glasses, place a rounded Tablespoon of yogurt in the bottom of each glass. Add about a teaspoon of fresh fruit and then a rounded teaspoon of granola. Repeat layers until the glass is almost full, ending with yogurt. Top with a slice of star fruit or kiwi, a sprig of mint and a pinch of granola.

Cherry Granola:
Combine oats, walnuts and coconut in a lightly greased 9 x 13 x 2-inch baking pan; set aside. In a saucepan over medium heat, combine syrups and cinnamon; bring to a boil. Remove from heat; stir in vanilla.

Pour over oat mixture and toss to coat. Bake at 275° for 30 minutes or until golden brown, stirring every 10 minutes. Cool and add cherries.

Store in airtight container. Yields about 2 cups of granola.

Grey Hare Inn, Vineyard Bed & Breakfast

1994 Carroll Road
Old Mission Peninsula
P.O. Box 1535
Traverse City, MI 49685
(231)947-2214
www.pentel.net/greyhare
greyhare@pentel.net

Hosts: Cindy and Jay Ruzak

The Grey Hare Inn is a working vineyard located in the heart of Northern Michigan's wine country, offering a hospitality style typical of a southern France farmhouse. The locally renowned full gourmet breakfast prepares guests for a day filled with wine tasting, sailing, biking, golfing, skiing, hiking and shopping.

Rates at the Grey Hare Inn, Vineyard range from $115-$185.
Rates include a full gourmet breakfast.

Tuscan Breakfast Strata

While the Grey Hare Inn is reminiscent of a southern France farmhouse, many of the Provencal recipes used are very Tuscan in nature as well. This recipe was chosen because it can be used for a larger crowd or with minor variations for individual portions as served at our Bed and Breakfast.

serves 6 or 12

---

2 pounds nonfat cottage cheese
2 medium yellow onions, finely chopped
2 packages (10 ounces each) frozen chopped
      spinach, thawed and squeezed dry or
      2 pounds fresh spinach
1/2 teaspoon salt
Tomato sauce (recipe follows)
12 ounces grated skim mozzarella cheese
4 egg whites

1/2 cup shredded Parmesan cheese
1 Tablespoon olive oil
4 cups thinly sliced mushrooms
1/4 teaspoon nutmeg
1/2 teaspoon pepper
1 pound day old French bread, sliced ¼" thick
4 whole eggs
2 cups nonfat milk
1/2 cup minced fresh parsley

3 medium mixing bowls
2- 8 x 12-inch lasagna pans or 8 individual soufflé dishes
Baking Time: 1 hour
Baking Temperature: 375°

Spray two 8 x 12 inch lasagna pans with nonstick cooking spray. Line a footed colander with a double thickness of cheesecloth. Set the colander into a bowl. Spoon the cottage cheese into the cheesecloth. Set aside to drain. Heat 1/2 Tablespoon oil in a nonstick skillet. Sauté onions over low heat until soft (about 8-10 minutes). Put onions into a large bowl; set aside.

Heat remaining 1/2 Tablespoon oil in same skillet. Increase heat to medium high and sauté mushrooms until moisture has evaporated (about 8-10 minutes). Put mushrooms in bowl with onions. Squeeze cheesecloth to remove any excess liquid and put cottage cheese in bowl with spinach, salt, pepper and nutmeg. Spoon 1/4 of the tomato sauce into the bottom of each of the prepared pans (using a total of 1/2 of the sauce). Arrange 1/4 of the bread pieces on top of the sauce in each pan. Divide the spinach mixture between the two pans, then place another layer of the bread on top of the spinach mixture. Sprinkle the onion – mushroom mixture over the second layer of bread. Divide the mozzarella cheese between the two pans, then top with remaining tomato sauce.

In another bowl, beat together the eggs, egg whites and milk. Slowly pour half of the mixture over each strata. Use a knife to gently cut into the layers to allow them to absorb the egg mixture. Cover with plastic wrap and refrigerate overnight.

When ready to cook, unwrap and place in a preheated 375° oven for 40 minutes. Sprinkle with Parmesan cheese and return to the oven for another 15 minutes or until the stratas are golden brown and knife inserted in the center comes out clean. Let stand 10 minutes before cutting to serve. Each strata serves 6.

Tomato Sauce:
1 Tablespoon olive oil
3 garlic cloves
2 bay leaves
1/2 teaspoon dried oregano
3 Tablespoons fresh parsley, chopped
1 onion, coarsely chopped

2 cans plum tomatoes, drained and diced
1/2 teaspoon dried thyme
1 teaspoon dried basil
1/4 teaspoon salt
1/4 teaspoon pepper

Heat the oil in a nonstick skillet and sauté onions until soft (about 5-6 minutes). Add garlic and sauté for 2-3 minutes. Add tomatoes, bay leaves, thyme, oregano, basil; simmer for 15-20 minutes. Remove bay leaves; add parsley, salt, and pepper. Set aside to cool.

White Swan Inn

303 South Mears Avenue
Whitehall, MI 49461
(231)894-5169 or (888)948-7926
www.whiteswaninn.com
info@whiteswaninn.com

Hosts: Cathy and Ron Russell

Gracious hospitality in a relaxing setting is the hallmark of the White Swan Inn. Guests enjoy spacious and delightfully decorated bedrooms with private baths. The beautiful Cygnet Suite with its elegant whirlpool tub pampers the senses. A large screened porch filled with white wicker furniture is the perfect spot to read a favorite novel or just watch the world go by.

The White Swan Inn is located in the wonderful resort area of White Lake. The beauty of Lake Michigan, the forests and dunes enhance the area; every season offers a variety of outdoor activities as well as theater, concerts and museums. The White Swan Inn is within walking distance of shops, dining and White Lake; bring your bikes for a trip on the Hart-Montague Bike Trail.

Visit the White Swan Inn once and you will return again and again.

Rates at the White Swan Inn range from $95-$155.
Rates include a full breakfast.

3 Cheese Spinach Quiche

Many more guests at the White Swan Inn are requesting vegetarian entrées. This delicious quiche fills the bill nicely, and I can honor their request without skimping on flavor. I complement the quiche with a fresh fruit medley, warm scones or muffins, and freshly squeezed juice. Guaranteed to give your guests or family a healthy start to the day.

serves 6

---

1 box (10 ounces) chopped frozen spinach, thawed
4 ounces Swiss cheese, shredded
4 Tablespoons Parmesan cheese, grated
1 container (15 ounces) Ricotta cheese, regular, lite or fat-free
4 ounces sliced mushrooms (fresh are best)
4 eggs or equivalent egg beaters
2/3 cup milk
1 Tablespoon dried minced onion
1/2 teaspoon salt
1/4 teaspoon pepper
1/4 teaspoon ground nutmeg
1 unbaked 9-inch pie shell, refrigerated or frozen

1 small mixing bowl
1 large mixing bowl
1 9-inch pie plate
Baking Time: 1 hour
Baking Temperature: 375°

Preheat oven to 375°.

Thoroughly drain thawed spinach. Mix drained spinach, Swiss cheese, Parmesan cheese and Ricotta cheese in large mixing bowl. Gently stir in mushrooms. In a small mixing bowl, whisk together eggs, milk, onion and seasonings. Add egg mixture to spinach mixture; gently stir together. Pour into unbaked pie shell. Place on baking sheet in case the filling overflows.

Bake for 1 hour or until knife inserted in center comes out clean. Let the quiche set for 5 minutes before cutting.

Tropical Muffins

Reminiscent of the Caribbean islands, these moist muffins always delight our guests. The scent of fresh baked muffins is a special treat. Create a little magic for your family or guests each morning!

makes 10-12 muffins

---

1 1/2 cups all-purpose flour
3/4 cup chopped pecans
3/4 cup sugar
1 1/2 teaspoons baking powder
1 egg, lightly beaten
2/3 cup sour cream
1/2 cup butter or margarine, melted
1 teaspoon vanilla extract or rum extract
1 can (8 ounces) crushed pineapple, drained
2/3 cup flaked coconut

1 small mixing bowl
1 large mixing bowl
1 standard size muffin tin
Baking Time: 18-22 minutes
Baking Temperature: 400°

Preheat oven to 400°. In a large mixing bowl, combine flour, pecans, sugar and baking powder.

Combine egg, sour cream, butter and vanilla or rum extract in a small mixing bowl; mix well.

Stir egg mixture into dry ingredients just until moistened. Gently fold in pineapple and coconut.

Fill paper-lined muffin cups 3/4 full. Bake at 400° for 18-22 minutes or until muffins test done.

Remove from muffin tin and cool on a wire rack.

Another great recipe from White Swan Inn.....

Best Ever Brownies

Greet family and guests with the delicious scent of chocolate when they arrive at your door. These brownies will disappear nearly as fast as you can bake them. Make up several batches of the dry mix, label and store in large Ziploc bags. When you need a quick dessert, just melt butter, stir in eggs and vanilla and pop into the oven.

makes one 7 x 12 or 9 x 13 inch pan

---

1 1/3 cups all-purpose flour
1/2 cup cocoa
2/3 cup sugar
2/3 cup brown sugar, packed
1/2 teaspoon salt
1/2 teaspoon baking powder
1/2 cup semi-sweet chocolate chips
1/2 cup vanilla chips
1/2 cup pecans or walnuts, chopped
1/2 cup butter or margarine, melted
1 teaspoon vanilla
3 eggs

1 large mixing bowl
1- 7 x 12-inch or 9 x 13-inch baking dish
Baking Time: 30-35 minutes
Baking Temperature: 350°

Preheat oven to 350°. In a large mixing bowl, combine flour, cocoa, sugars, salt, baking powder, chocolate chips, vanilla chips and nuts.

Stir butter, vanilla and eggs into dry ingredients just until blended. Do not overmix.

Pour into greased 7 x 12-inch or 9 x 13-inch baking pan. Spread evenly.

Bake at 350° for 30-35 minutes. Do not overbake.

Cool in pan on wire rack. When cool, cut into desired pieces. Enjoy!

Country Hermitage Bed & Breakfast

7710 US 31 North
Williamsburg, MI 49690
(231)938-5930
www.countryhermitage.com
reservations@countryhermitage.com

Hosts: Nels and Michelle Veliquette

Our mission is to provide our guests with a pleasant, comfortable experience and delicious culinary delights! Country Hermitage Bed & Breakfast is located on a 250-acre working cherry farm overlooking East Grand Traverse Bay. This Victorian style farmhouse was built in 1883 by a pioneer of the region from its earliest days. Each of the five large guest rooms has a spectacular view of the bay and surrounding cherry orchards.

Guest rooms feature their own unique décor, private bath, television and central air conditioning. Our luxury suites offer in-room fireplaces and spa style tubs. Country Hermitage is perfect for your most romantic getaway in any season!

Rates at Country Hermitage range from $110-$180.
Rates include a full breakfast.

Cherry Country Scones

This recipe makes light and delicious scones. The key to preparing this recipe is to prevent the butter from breaking down. Keep the batter refrigerated if you won't be baking them all at once. This early morning starter is a tasty treat at any time throughout the day, especially tea time!

makes a baker's dozen

---

2 cups flour
1 Tablespoon sugar
1/2 teaspoon baking soda
1 teaspoon baking powder
pinch of salt
2/3 cup buttermilk
2 eggs
1 teaspoon vanilla extract
2/3 cup chopped dried cherries
3/4 cup grated frozen butter
powdered sugar

1 large mixing bowl
1 medium mixing bowl
1 cookie sheet
Baking Time: 16-19 minutes
Baking Temperature: 375°

Preheat oven to 375°.

In a large mixing bowl, combine flour, sugar, baking soda, baking powder and salt. In a medium mixing bowl, whisk eggs, buttermilk and vanilla extract. Cut frozen grated butter into the flour mixture with a pastry mixer until thoroughly combined. Add egg mixture until dough forms. Fold in the chopped cherries and spoon finished dough onto cookie sheet (approximately 3 Tablespoons per scone).

Bake at 375° for 16-19 minutes or until golden brown. Remove from oven and place scones on rack.

Sprinkle with powdered sugar and serve warm.

Topliff's Tara
Bed & Breakfast, LLC

251 Noble Road
Williamston, MI 48895
(517)655-8860 or (800)251-1607
www.topliffstara.com
info@topliffstara.com

Hosts: Don and Sheryl Topliff

A 50-acre llama farm provides the backdrop for this stately country Bed & Breakfast. Located just 10 minutes from the campus of Michigan State University and even closer to charming downtown Williamston, the Meridian Mall, and numerous golf courses and restaurants, visitors can enjoy both serenity and convenience. Each of the five bedrooms is uniquely custom decorated to reflect the favorite pastimes of the innkeepers. Topliff's Tara is exceptionally suited to small gatherings of friends or family (up to 11 persons), since the innkeepers' living quarters are separate from the guest areas. The Bed & Breakfast portion of the home was built in 1905 and renovated for the Bed & Breakfast opening in 2000. Handcrafted items, including dried floral and llama fiber products, are available for guests to purchase in the first floor gift shop. For a memorable, relaxing getaway, Tara will steal your heart.

Rates at Topliff's Tara range from $75-$125.
Rates include a full breakfast.

Rhubarb Bread

This recipe uses rhubarb, one of the most readily available, easy to harvest, and simple to preserve fruits in Michigan. While it is called bread, it really is more like a coffee cake and can, in fact, be made in a bundt pan. It is best served warm. Guests always rave about it and request the recipe.

makes 2 medium loaves or 1 bundt pan, approximately 12 servings

---

3/4 cup brown sugar
3/4 cup granulated sugar
2/3 cup vegetable oil
1 egg
3 cups flour
1 teaspoon baking soda
1/2 teaspoon salt
1 cup sour cream
1 teaspoon vanilla
2 cups rhubarb, diced
1/2 cup pecans, chopped

Topping:
1/2 cup brown sugar
1/2 teaspoon cinnamon
1 Tablespoon butter

1 small mixing bowl
1 medium mixing bowl
1 large mixing bowl
2 medium bread pans or 1 bundt pan
2 bread trays
Baking Time: 55-60 minutes
Baking Temperature: 350°

Preheat oven to 350°. Thoroughly mix together sugars, oil and egg in large mixing bowl. Sift together flour, baking soda and salt in a medium mixing bowl. Combine sour cream and vanilla. Alternately add flour mixture and sour cream mixture to sugar mixture. Blend in rhubarb and pecans. Pour into greased and floured bundt pan or 2 medium bread pans. Sprinkle with topping.

Bake 55-60 minutes. Cool 10 minutes before removing from pan.

Topping:
Cut butter into brown sugar and cinnamon to make fine crumbs.

Apple-Nut Coffee Cake

My niece Diane, who works for the Michigan Apple Committee, would never forgive me if I did not include a recipe with Michigan apples! I tried recipe after recipe in search of the one for the perfect apple coffee cake. It has just the texture and flavor I was looking for. Our good friends, Terry and Renee Wortz, gave us the recipe. They are now serving in the Christian/ medical missionary field for the Mission Society for United Methodists. I am reminded of them every time I bake this.

makes one cake

1/2 cup shortening
1 cup sugar
2 eggs
1 teaspoon vanilla
2 cups flour
1/4 teaspoon salt
1 teaspoon baking soda
1 cup sour cream
2 cups diced apples

Topping:
1/2 cup chopped pecans
1/2 cup brown sugar
1 teaspoon ground cinnamon
2 Tablespoons melted butter

1 medium mixing bowl
1 large mixing bowl
1- 9 x 13-inch pan
Baking Time: 35-40 minutes
Baking Temperature: 350°

Preheat oven to 350°. In a large mixing bowl, cream together shortening and sugar. Add eggs and vanilla. Beat well. Stir in flour, salt and baking soda. Add sour cream. Fold in apples. Spread in a well-greased 9 x 13 x 2-inch pan.

Bake at 350° for 35-40 minutes or until toothpick comes out clean.

Topping:
Combine all ingredients in a medium mixing bowl. Sprinkle over batter.

Another great recipe from Topliff's Tara Bed & Breakfast...

Cherry Cheese French Toast

This recipe features tart dried cherries, a favorite Michigan fruit. It is not easy to discern whether you are having a nourishing breakfast or enjoying a mouth-watering dessert. Chocolate muffins are an excellent complement to this main course.

serves 6 (2 slices each)

---

12 slices French bread, bias cut 1 1/2 inches thick
1 cup dried tart cherries
1/2 cup rum
1 egg
4 Tablespoons mascarpone cheese
1 Tablespoon confectioner's sugar

Egg Mixture:
2 eggs, beaten
1 1/2 cups milk
2 teaspoons vanilla extract
2 teaspoons ground cinnamon
1 teaspoon grated nutmeg

Buttered Cherry Sauce:
1/2 cup reserved dried tart cherries
1/4 cup butter
2 cups cranberry juice
2 Tablespoons granulated sugar
2 Tablespoons cornstarch
2 Tablespoons water

1 small mixing bowl
1 medium mixing bowl
1 small saucepan
1 griddle
1 sheet pan
1 large platter
Baking Time: 20 minutes
Baking Temperature: 350°

Cut a pocket through the side of each slice of bread. Combine dried cherries and rum in a small saucepan. Simmer, covered, for 5 minutes or until cherries are soft and rum is almost evaporated. Combine 1 egg, mascarpone cheese, sugar and 1/2 cup softened cherries in a small mixing bowl. Mix well. Reserve remaining 1/2 cup cherries for buttered cherry sauce. Spoon cherry-cheese mixture into pockets of bread slices. Cover and chill, if desired.

Egg Mixture:
Combine egg, milk, vanilla, cinnamon and nutmeg in a large mixing bowl. Mix well.

Generously butter preheated 350° griddle. Dip stuffed bread slices into egg mixture, then transfer to hot griddle. Cook until golden brown on both sides. Transfer to sheet pan sprayed with nonstick cooking spray.

Bake in a preheated 350° oven for 20 minutes or until bread slices are puffed and filling is hot. Top each side of French toast with buttered cherry sauce.

Buttered Cherry Sauce:
Prepare topping while French toast is baking. In saucepan, combine reserved cherries, butter, cranberry juice and sugar. Simmer, stirring occasionally, until butter is melted. Combine cornstarch and water. Add cornstarch mixture slowly to hot cherry mixture, whisking constantly. Increase heat and bring to a boil, stirring often, until thickened. Reduce heat. Simmer for about 5 minutes.

Serve over Cherry Cheese French Toast.

Parish House Inn

103 South Huron Street
Ypsilanti, MI 48197
(734)480-4800
www.parishhouseinn.com
parishinn@aol.com

Hosts: Chris and Lance Mason

Originally the parsonage for the First Congregational Church, this Queen Anne house was moved to its current location in 1987, enlarged and totally restored. Step inside and you are wrapped in Victorian elegance, in antiques, in ceiling fans and graceful tulip fixtures plus the aroma of the full breakfast. Off the narrow high ceiling hallways are the eight guest rooms, each with private bath, television, VCR and telephone with modem. We are located in Ypsilanti's Historic District and are one mile from Eastern Michigan University and one half mile from I-94.

Rates at Parish House Inn range from $95-$150.
Rates include a full breakfast.

Dairy Free Pumpkin Nut Bread

The chewy texture and spicy flavor of this pumpkin bread delights the taste buds of all of our guests. It is especially nice, however, to serve when guests have allergies to eggs and dairy products or are vegans.

makes one loaf

2 1/2 cups all-purpose flour
2 cups sugar
2 teaspoons baking soda
1/2 teaspoon ground cinnamon
1/2 teaspoon ground ginger
1/2 teaspoon ground allspice
1/2 teaspoon salt
1 3/4 cups canned solid pack pumpkin
1/2 cup vegetable oil
1 cup chopped nuts

1 medium mixing bowl
1 large mixing bowl
1 9x3-inch loaf pan or 3 mini loaf pans
Baking Time: 60 minutes for 9x3-inch pan; 45 minutes for mini pans
Baking Temperature: 350°

Preheat oven to 350°. Coat pan(s) with nonstick cooking spray.

In a medium mixing bowl, combine flour, sugar, baking soda, ground cinnamon, ground ginger, ground allspice and salt.

In a large mixing bowl, mix together pumpkin, oil and nuts.

Stir the dry ingredients into the pumpkin mixture (batter will be thick). Divide batter among pans, if necessary.

Bake until tester inserted in center comes out clean or top springs back when touched, about 60 minutes for a large loaf and 45 minutes for mini pans.

Directory of the Michigan Lake to Lake Bed & Breakfast Association

Adrian	Briar Oaks Inn	517-263-7501 www.briaroaksinn.com
Algonac	Linda's Lighthouse Inn	810-794-2992 www.lindasbnb.com
Allegan	**Castle in the Country B&B**	**888-673-8054 www.castleinthecountry.com**
Allegan	Delano Inn Victorian B&B, The	866-686-0240 www.delanoinn.com
Allegan	Inn at Froggy's Pond	888-686-2212 www.froggys.com
Alma	**Saravilla**	**989-463-4078 www.saravilla.com**
Ann Arbor	Urban Retreat Bed & Breakfast	734-971-8110 www.theurbanretreat.com
Arcadia	**Arcadia House**	**231-889-4394 www.thearcadiahouse.com**
Atlanta	Briley Inn B&B	989-785-4784 www.yesmichigan.com/brileyinn
Auburn Hills	Cobblestone Manor Luxury Historic Inn	800-370-7270 www.cobblestonemanor.com
AuTrain	Pinewood Lodge B&B	906-892-8300 www.pinewoodlodgebnb.com
Battle Creek	Greencrest Manor	269-962-8633 www.greencrestmanor.com/
Bay City	Clements Inn	800-442-4605 www.laketolake.com/clementsinn
Bay City	**Keswick Manor**	**989-893-6598 www.keswickmanor.com**
Bay View	Gingerbread House	231-347-3538 www.gingerbreadbb.com
Bellaire	Bellaire Bed and Breakfast	800-545-0780 www.bellairebandb.com
Bellaire	Grand Victorian	800-336-3860 www.grandvictorian.com
Bellaire	Stone Waters Inn ... On the River	800-336-3860 www.stonewatersinn.com
Beulah	**Elliott House**	**231-882-7075 www.elliottbbb.com**
Big Bay	Big Bay Point Lighthouse Bed and Breakfast	906-345-9957 www.bigbaylighthouse.com
Boyne City	Deer Lake B&B	231-582-9039 www.deerlakebb.com
Brighton	Canterbury Chateau	810-516-2120 www.laketolake.com/canterbury/index.htm
Brooklyn	Chicago Street Inn	517-592-3888 www.chicagostreetinn.com
Brooklyn	**Dewey Lake Manor**	**800-815-5253 www.bbonline.com/mi/deweylake**
Burt Lake	Rohn House & Farm	888-895-7411 http://my.freeway.net/~rohnhous
Calumet	Belknap's Garnet House	906-337-5607 www.laketolake.com/garnet-house/index.htm
Cedarville	Les Cheneaux Inn B&B	906-484-2007 www.laketolake.com/lescheneaux/index.htm
Central Lake	Bridgewalk B&B	231-544-8122 www.bridgewalkbandb.com
Central Lake	Moonkeeper B & B	800-942-6858 www.moonkeeperbb.com
Charlevoix	Aaron's Windy Hill Guest Lodge	231-547-2804 www.aaron'swindyhill.com
Charlevoix	Charlevoix Country Inn	231-547-5134 www.charlevoixcountryinn.com
Charlevoix	Horton Creek Inn B&B	866-582-5373 www.hortoncreekinnbb.com
Cheboygan	Gables Bed and Breakfast	231-627-5079 www.mich-web.com/gablesbb/
Chelsea	**Waterloo Gardens Bed & Breakfast**	**734-433-1612 ww.waterloogardensbb.com**
Chesaning	Stone House Bed & Breakfast	989-845-4440 www.stonehousebnb.com
Clark Lake	Claddagh B&B	517-768-1000 www.getaway2smi.com/claddagh/index.htm
Clarkston	Millpond Inn	800-867-4142 www.laketolake.com/millpond/index.htm
Clio	**Cinnamon Stick Farm B&B**	**810-686-8391 www.cinnamonstickfarmbnb.com**
Coleman	Buttonville Inn	989-465-9364 www.buttonvilleinn.com
Constantine	Inn at Constantine	800-435-5365 www.innatconstantine.com
East Lansing	Wild Goose Inn	517-241-7451 www.laketolake.com/wildgoose/index.htm
East Tawas	**East Tawas Junction B&B**	**989-362-8006 www.east-tawas.com**
Elk Rapids	**Cairn House B&B**	**231-264-8994 www.cairnhouse.com**
Ellsworth	**House on the Hill**	**231-588-6304 www.thehouseonthehill.com**
Ellsworth	Lake Michigan's Abiding Place	231-599-2808 www.abidingplace.com
Fennville	Hidden Pond B&B	269-561-2491 www.laketolake.com/hidden/index.htm
Fennville	**Kingsley House**	**269-561-6425 www.kingsleyhouse.com**
Frankenmuth	**Bavarian Town Bed & Breakfast**	**989-652-8057 www.laketolake.com/bavarian**
Frankenmuth	Frankenmuth Bed & Breakfast	989-652-8897 www.laketolake.com/Frankenmuth/index.htm
Frankfort	Stonewall Inn	231-352-9299 www.stonewallinnbb.com/
Frankfort	Windchime Inn	866-352-9450 www.windchimeinn.com
Fruitport	Village Park B&B	800-469-1118 www.bbonline.com/mi/villagepark
Gladstone	**Kipling House**	**877-905-7776 www.kiplinghouse.com**
Glen Arbor	Glen Arbor B & B	877-253-4200 www.glenarborbandb.com
Glen Arbor	Sylvan Inn	231-334-4333 www.sylvaninn.com
Grand Haven	Boyden House Bed & Breakfast	877-844-0123 www.bbonline.com/mi/boyden
Grand Haven	Looking Glass Inn	800-951-6427 www.bbonline.com/mi/lookingglass
Grand Rapids	Madison Street Inn	800-618-5615 www.laketolake.com/madison/index.htm
Grandville	Prairieside Suites	616-538-9440 www.prairiesidesuites.com/

Grass Lake	Coppy's Inn 517-522-4850 www.bbonline.com/mi/coppys
Grayling	Borchers Au Sable Bed & Breakfast 800-762-8756 www.canoeborchers.com
Grayling	Hanson House Bed & Breakfast 989-348-6630 wwwhansonhousebandb.com
Gulliver	Thistledowne at Seul Choix 800-522-4649 www.thistledowne.com
Harbor Beach	**State Street Inn 866-424-7961 www.thestatestreetinn.com**
Harrison	Carriage House Inn 989-539-1300 www.carriagehouseinn.com
Hart	Rooms at The Inn B&B 877-659-6555 www.roomsattheinn.com
Hartland	Farmstead B&B 248-887-6086 www.laketolake.com/farmstead/index.htm
Hastings	**Adrounie House B & B 800-927-8505 www.adrounie.com**
Holland	Dutch Colonial Inn 616-396-3664 www.dutchcolonialinn.com
Holland	**Inn at Old Orchard Road 616-335-2525**
	www.bbonline.com/mi/orchardroad
Holland	**Shaded Oaks B&B 616-399-4194 www.shadedoaks.com**
Holland	**Thistle Inn 616-399-0409 www.bbonline.com/mi/thistleinn/index.htm**
Holly	Holly Crossing B&B 800-556-2262 www.hollybandb.com
Interlochen	Hall Creek B&B 231-263-2560 www.hallcreek.com
Interlochen	Lake 'N Pines Lodge 231-275-6671 www.2mm.com/lake
Ithaca	Bon Accord Farm B&B 989-875-3136 www.bonaccordfarm.com
Jackson	Rose Trellis Bed & Breakfast 517-787-2035 www.rosetrellisbhcom
Jonesville	Horse & Carriage B&B 517-849-2732 www.hcbnb.com
Jonesville	Munro House 800-320-3792 www.munrohouse.com
Kalamazoo	**Hall House B&B 888-761-2525 www.hallhouse.com**
Kalamazoo	Stuart Avenue Inn 800-461-0621 www.stuartaveinn.com
Lakeside	Pebble House Bed and Breakfast 269-469-1416 www.thepebblehouse.com
Lakeside	White Rabbit Inn 800-967-2224 www.whiterabbitinn.com
Laurium	Laurium Manor Inn 906-337-2549 www.lauriummanorinn.com
Leland	**Aspen House 800-762-7736 www.aspenhouseleland.com**
Leland	Centennial Inn 231-271-6460 www.laketolake.com/centennial/index.htm
Leland	Highlands of Leland 231-256-7632 www.highlandsofleland.com
Leland	Manitou Manor 231-256-7712 www.bbhost.com/manitoumanorbb
Leland	Snowbird Inn 231-256-9773 www.snowbirdinn.com
Lewiston	Gorton House 989-786-2764 www.gortonhouse.com
Lexington	Governor's Inn 888-909-5770 www.governorsinnbnb.com
Lexington	Inn the Garden B&B 810-359-8966 www.inngarden.com
Lexington	Powell House B&B 810-359-5533 www.laketolake.com/powell/index.htm
Lowell	**McGee Homestead 616-897-8142 www.iserv.net/~mcgeebb**
Ludington	Abbey Lynn Inn B&B 800-795-5421 www.bbonline.com/mi/abbeylynn
Ludington	Bed & Breakfast at Ludington 231-843-9768 www.carrinter.net/bedbkfst
Ludington	Inn At Ludington 800-845-9170 www.inn-ludington.com
Ludington	**Lamplighter B&B 800-301-9792 www.ludington-michigan.com**
Ludington	Summit Inn 231-843-4052 www.jackpine.com/~summitinn
Mackinac Island	Bay View B&B 906-847-3295 www.mackinacbayview.com/
Mackinac Island	Cottage Inn of Mackinac 231-922-9165 www.cottageinofMackinac.com
Mackinac Island	Haan's 1830 Inn 906-847-6244 www.mackinac.com/haans
Mackinac Island	Metivier Inn 888-695-6562 www.metivier.com
Mackinaw City	Deer Head Lodge 231-436-3337 www.deerhead.com
Manistee	Manistee Country House 231-723-2367
	www.laketolake.com/manistee/index.htm
Manistee	**Morningside Manor Bed & Breakfast 888-419-9668**
	www.morningsidebnb.com
Manistique	**Royal Rose Bed & Breakfast 906-341-4886**
	www.manistique.com/bed_brkf/royalrose/home.htm
Marine City	**Heather House 810-765-3175 www.bluewatertoday.com/heatherhouse**
Marlette	Country View B&B 989-635-2468 www.laketolake.com/countryview/index.htm
Marshall	Joy House B&B 269-789-1323 www.kephart.com/joyhouse
Marshall	**National House Inn 269-781-7374 www.nationalhouseinn.com**
Mears	Dunes Bed & Breakfast 866-331-0033 www.bbonline.com/mi/thedunes
Mio	Teaspoon B&B 989-826-3889 www.teaspoonbb.com
Monroe	Lotus Bed and Breakfast 734-735-1077 www.laketolake.com/lotus/index.htm
Mt. Pleasant	Country Chalet/Edelweiss Haus 877-878-9259 www.countrychalet.net
Muskegon	Hackley-Holt House B&B 888-271-5609 www.bbonline.com/mi/hhhbb
Muskegon	**Port City Victorian Inn 800-274-3574 www.portcityinn.com**
National City	Good Tour Bed and Breakfast 989-362-7047 www.goodtourbnb.com
New Buffalo	Tall Oaks Inn 800-936-0034 www.harborcountry.com/guide/talloaks
Newberry	MacLeod House 906-293-3841 www.macleodhouse.com

Northport	Old Mill Pond Inn 231-386-7341 www.laketolake.com/oldmillpond/index.htm
Northville	Fraser Inn 248-349-8809 www.thefraserinn.com
Oden	Inn at Crooked Lake 231-439-9984 www.innatcrookedlake.com
Omena	Frieda's B & B 231-386-7274 www.laketolake.com/frieda/index.htm
Omena	**Lisa's Northwoods Bed and Breakfast 231-271-2010**
	www.leelanau.com/northwoods
Omena	Omena Sunset Lodge B & B 231-386-9080 www.omenasunsetlodge.com
Onekama	**Canfield House 231-889-5756 www.thecanfieldhouse.com**
Ontonagon	Northern Light Inn 800-238-0018 www.laketolake.com/northernlight
Oscoda	**Huron House 989-739-9255 www.huronhouse.com**
Oscoda	Manor House Inn 989-739-1977 www.manorhouse-oscoda.com
Pentwater	**Candlewyck House 231-869-5967 www.Candlewyckhouse.com**
Pentwater	Historic Nickerson Inn 800-742-1288 www.nickersoninn.com
Pentwater	**Pentwater Abbey B&B 877-720-4850 www.bbonline.com/mi/abbey/**
Perry	Cobb House 517-625-7443 www.laketolake.com/cobb/index.htm
Petoskey	510 Elizabeth 800-484-8027 www.laketolake.com/elizabeth/index.htm
Petoskey	Ambrosia Bed & Breakfast 800-601-1064 www.ambrosiabb.com
Petoskey	**Serenity A Bed & Breakfast 877-347-6171 www.serenitybb.com**
Pinckney	Bunn-Pher Hill Bed & Breakfast 734-878-9236 www.laketolake.com/bunn/index.htm
Pleasant Lake	Hankerd Inn 517-769-6153 my.voyager.net/hankerd
Plymouth	**932 Penniman - A Bed & Breakfast 888-548-4887**
	www.bbonline.com/mi/penniman
Port Austin	Captain's Inn B&B 888-277-6631 www/laketolake.com/captains_inn/index.htm
Port Hope	**Stafford House Bed & Breakfast 989-428-4554 www.staffordhousepthope.com**
Port Huron	**Davidson House 810-987-3922 www.davidsonhouse.com**
Port Huron	Hill Estate Bed and Breakfast 877-982-8187 www.laketolake.com/hillestate
Port Sanilac	Holland's Little House in the Country 866-622-9739 www.connieholland.com
Port Sanilac	Raymond House Inn 800-622-7229 www.bbonline.com/mi/raymond
Prudenville	Springbrook Inn 989-366-6347 www.springbrookinn.com
Romeo	Brabb House B&B 586-752-4726 www.brabbhousebnb.com
Saginaw	Cousins B&B 989-790-1728 www.laketolake.com/cousins/index.htm
Saugatuck	Park House Inn 800-321-4535 www.parkhouseinn.com
Saugatuck	**Sherwood Forest B&B 800-838-1246 www.sherwoodforestbandb.com**
Saugatuck	**Twin Gables Inn 800-231-2185 www.twingablesinn.com**
Saugatuck	**Twin Oaks Inn 800-788-6188 www.bbonline.com/mi/twinoaks**
Saugatuck	Wickwood Inn 269-857-1097 www.wickwoodinn.com
Sebewaing	Antique Inn 989-883-9424 www.antiqueinn.com
Sebewaing	Rummel's Tree Haven B&B 989-883-2450 www.laketolake.com/treehaven/index.htm
South Haven	A Country Place B&B 269-637-5523 www.csi-net.net/acountryplace
South Haven	Carriage House at the Harbor 269-639-2161 www.carriagehouseharbor.com
South Haven	Inn at the Park 877-739-1776 www.innpark.com
South Haven	Last Resort, A B&B Inn 269-637-8943 www.lastresortinn.com/
South Haven	Sand Castle Inn 269-639-1110 www.thesandcastleinn.com
South Haven	Seymour House 269-227-3918 www.seymourhouse.com
South Haven	Victoria Resort B&B 800-473-7376 www.victoriaresort.com
South Haven	Yelton Manor 269-637-5220 www.yeltonmanor.com
Spring Lake	Seascape B&B 616-842-8409 www.bbonline.com/mi/seascape
St. Clair	**William Hopkins Manor 810-329-0188 www.members.aol.com/whmanor/**
St. Joseph	Chestnut House 269-983-7413 www.bbonline.com/mi/chestnut

St. Joseph	**South Cliff Inn 269-983-4881 www.southcliffinn.com**
Stanton	Hotel Montcalm Bed & Breakfast 989-831-5055
	www.laketolake.com/hotelmontcalm/index.htm
Stanwood	Outback Lodge & Stables 231-972-7255
	www.laketolake.com/outback_lodge/index.htm
Sturgis	Hidden Hill 800-220-5601 www.laketolake.com/hiddenhill/index.htm
Suttons Bay	**Inn at Black Star Farms 231-271-4886 www.blackstarfarms.com**
Suttons Bay	**Korner Kottage B&B 231-271-2711 www.kornerkottage.com**
Suttons Bay	Morning Glory Beach 231-271-6047 www.laketolake.com/morning/index.htm
Traverse City	**Aberdeen Stone Cottage 231-935-3715 www.aberdeenstonecottage.com**
Traverse City	Bears' Den Bed and Breakfast 231-932-1488 www.bearsdentc.com
Traverse City	Bowers Harbor B&B 231-223-7869 www.bowersharborbb.com
Traverse City	**Country Hermitage Bed and Breakfast 231-938-5930**
	www.countryhermitage.com
Traverse City	**Field of Dreams Bed and Breakfast 231-223-7686**
	www.pentel.net/fieldofdreams
Traverse City	**Grey Hare Inn, Vineyard B&B 800-873-0652 www.pentel.net/greyhare**
Traverse City	Linden Lea on Long Lake 231-943-9182 www.lindenleabb.com
Traverse City	Neahtawanta Inn 231-223-7315 www.oldmission.com/inn
Union	Union House Bed and Breakfast 269-641-9988
	www.laketolake.com/unionhouse/index.htm
Union Pier	Garden Grove B&B 800-613-2872 www.gardengrove.net
Union Pier	Rivers Edge Bed & Breakfast 800-742-0592 www.riversedgebandb.com
Vanderbilt	Hoods In The Woods B & B 231-549-2560
	www.laketolake.com/hoods/index.htm
Waterford	Carriage House Bed & Breakfast 248-623-0025 www.waterfordcarriage.com
Webberville	Basic Brewer Bed & Breakfast 800-468-3951
	www.laketolake.com/basic/index.htm
Whitehall	**White Swan Inn B&B 888-948-7926 www.whiteswaninn.com**
Williamston	**Topliff's Tara Bed and Breakfast 517-655-8860 www.topliffstara.com**
Yale	Roush House 810-387-2810 www.theroushhouse.com/
Ypsilanti	**Parish House Inn 800-480-4866 www.parishhouseinn.com**

Index of Recipes

To order additional copies of
Great Lakes, Great Breakfasts

as well as other books in the Bed & Breakfast series

or for a FREE catalog of books
from The Guest Cottage, Inc., contact:

The Guest Cottage, Inc.

PO Box 848
Woodruff, WI 54568
phone: 800-333-8122
fax: 715-358-9456
e-mail: amherst@newnorth.net